Schuylkill

Valley

Journal

Volume 54
Spring/Summer 2022

Patrons of *Schuylkill Valley Journal*

(contributions of $100 or more)

Subscriptions:

Single Issue:	$18 (includes mailing)
1 year:	$33 (includes mailing)
2 years:	$58 (includes mailing)

Submissions: See page 174 for a complete list of guidelines.

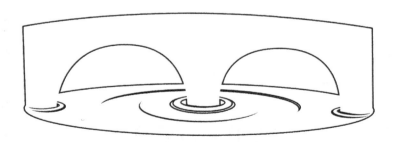

Cover image: Medicine Man
Sculptor: Cyrus Dallin, 1899
Photographer: Ron Howard

Founding Editor . . . . Jim Marinell

Publisher and Editor-in-Chief . . . . .Peter Krok

Poetry Editors . . . . Mary Jo LoBello Jerome
. . . . Jane Edna Mohler

Fiction Editor . . . . Fran Metzman

Flash Fiction Editor . . . . M.J. Iuppa

Creative Non-Fiction Editor. . . . . .Rob Kaniuk

Non-Fiction Editor. . . . . .Peter Krok

Art Editor . . . . .David P. Kozinski

Feature Writer. . . . . Mike Cohen

Contributing Writer. . . . . Eric Greinke

Contributing Writer. . . . . .Joe Tyson

Editorial Assistant (Submissions Reader). . Jenna Geisinger

Online Architect/Producer . . . . Zoe Musselman

Staff Photographer . . . . .Ron Howard

Print Production Editor/Layout Design . . . . Ed Hart

Schuylkill Valley Journal is published twice a year,
and is also available online at
www.svjlit.com

Contents
Volume 54, Spring/Summer 2022

Non-Fiction

Creative Non-Fiction

Mike Cohen and Connie Swartzman

A VISIT TO THE MEDICINE MAN

"He isn't nude," Connie declares, as we locate the *Medicine Man*. "He's wearing a head-piece, and an impressive-looking one at that!" Cyrus Dallin's sculpture, *Medicine Man*, is the latest object of our statue chasing quest for the *Schuylkill Valley Journal*. Connie and I trek about the city chasing statues. We have put on quite a lot of mileage over the years, so are grateful that the sculptures generally stand their ground. In preparation for our foray, we did some preliminary research.

The statue was installed in Philadelphia's Fairmount Park in 1903 in a ceremony where Native American ethnologist, Francis La Flesche, was invited to speak. Commenting on the figure, La Flesche was quoted as saying: "The nudity is not without its significance; it typifies the utter helplessness of man, when his strength is contrasted with the power of the Great Spirit..."

But Connie is right. Even from a distance, we can see the horns of the head dress as we drive from the periphery of Fairmount Park, and take the winding path from 33rd and Dauphin Streets. At a glance, I can tell he is clothed, if not head to toe, at least head *and* toe with his head dress and moccasins. High on a horse that stands on an eight-and-a-half foot tall granite base, the medicine man sits, his uplifted right hand more than 16 feet in the air.

But despite the height of the monument, it is easily overlooked. The traffic passes by oblivious to the presence of a statue that might, in other times and places, draw a crowd of admirers.

With difficulty we manage to find a place where we can park at the side of the road. We then approach on foot to the isolated spot where the sculpture stands. Crossing the street toward him, we are stopped in our tracks as the medicine man calls, "Whoa! My people already suffered too much from white man's diseases. Before you come any closer, kindly put on your masks."

We obey, and are permitted to proceed. I am a bit reluctant under the watchful eyes of the austere figure. But Connie doesn't hesitate. In a moment she is standing by the base of the statue. She looks up, with a smile that lights her face despite the mask, and begins to chat with the medicine man. "My! What fine horns you have on! And they're complemented by the elegant eagle feathers trailing gracefully down your back. You certainly are a well-dressed man." The medicine man, not accustomed to such attentions, struggles to maintain his unpretentious demeanor, as my style-conscious wife continues to articulate. "I love what you've done with your hair. The long braids lend a balance to the look." The medicine man may never have been addressed in this way, but doesn't seem to mind. "Your style is daring," she continues, "but not overly so, the loincloth designed to cover just enough. And those moccasins! They're attractive yet appear so soft and comfortable! I wish I could wear a pair like that," Connie sighs, "but they wouldn't provide enough arch support."

Though the figure of the medicine man is not nude, the horse is: no bridle, no reins, no blanket, no saddle, no stirrups, no horse shoes. The animal travels light, with nothing but the rider on his back. "Speaking of support," Connie asks, "how can a person manage to stay on a horse with nothing but the horse itself to hold onto?" At this point, the medicine man can contain himself no longer. Not at all vain about his appearance, he takes great pride in horsemanship. "The Spanish brought horses to this land in the 1600's," he says. "The white man did not understand the noble beast like my people did. We developed a rapport with the animal, learned to blend our strength, agility, and balance with those of the horse. Our horses helped us with mobility, hunting, and holding the intruders at bay—at least for a while—until the white man managed to take our beloved horses away, and force us onto reservations."

There is deep sorrow in his face, but also strong resolve.

"It's shameful," I say to Connie, "what America has done to Native Americans. At least, the *Medicine Man* is here to attest to it."

"But he's been put here, in a hard to reach place where not many people will see him. And look," Connie goes on, "there's not even an engraving or a plaque to tell about him."

"I can speak for myself," declares *Medicine Man.*

* * *

We have visited other Native American figures for our *Schuylkill Valley Journal* sculpture articles. Among them is the limestone figure featured in our 2010 article, purported to represent Tedyuscung, a Lenape chief. However, its head dress is not Lenape at all, but typical of the peoples of the plains.

The fact that it was accepted to represent a group it does not resemble is indicative of the stereotyping and generalizing that went on in the melting pot of the European mind that lumped all natives together and misnamed them "Indians."

Tedyuscung was sculpted by John Massey Rhind, a Scot educated in Edinburgh. He later came to New York and settled in New Jersey, where he may never have seen a Lenape person. So the inaccuracy of his figure of Tedyuscung is understandable.

By contrast, *Medicine Man's* sculptor, Cyrus Dallin (1861-1944), was raised in Springville, Utah. Many of his childhood playmates were Native Americans. His early exposure to their culture left him with a reverence and fascination for the people and their ways.

Dallin's *Medicine Man* is a faithful rendition of a person of the Western plains. The head dress, complete with buffalo horns and eagle feathers, is characteristically Lakota, as are the moccasins. Cyrus Dallin knew his subject in style and substance. There is a striking depth of understanding in the way the sculptor portrayed a blend of strength and vulnerability in the demeanor and posture of his subject

The *Medicine Man* is identified by profession, which was, in his culture, a spiritual rather than a scientific calling. His was a highly respected position among the Lakota. This man of the loin-cloth bore the authority of the Great Spirit.

Though he is not representative of a specific named person, there is something quite personal about the *Medicine Man*. There is an authenticity to him that goes beyond apparel, an earnestness in his facial expression. Dallin rendered a very human figure. The *Medicine Man* is not only a symbol, but a man.

After more than a century, the bronze sculpture remains a testament to the endurance of a people who have been discounted by the conceit of "Manifest Destiny," the replacement theory that deems European domination the ultimate fate of America. Still the *Medicine Man* remains to represent the great spirit of people who persist against the odds. Here at this quiet intersection in the park remains this humble tribute to what is most fundamentally the American spirit.

* * *

The *Medicine Man*'s maker took to sculpture quite naturally. In his teens, Cyrus Dallin worked in his father's silver mine. When the miners brought up some white clay, Cyrus used the material to mold male and female heads. The locals were so impressed by his skill that they funded Dallin's artistic pursuits. He went to Boston in 1880 to study under the sculptor, Truman Bartlett.

In 1883, Cyrus won a competition in Boston to sculpt an equestrian figure of Paul Revere. However, as his work on the sculpture proceeded, difficulties arose. The selection committee balked at awarding a contract to a young, inexperienced Westerner. Even after he was given the contract, several revisions of the sculpture were rejected. Funding became problematic. Cyrus Dallin's *Paul Revere* did not become a reality until decades later, when his seventh version of the sculpture was finally accepted. The statue was installed in 1940. So, one of the first projects of Dallin's long career became one of his last accomplishments.

Between the start and finish of the *Paul Revere* project, Cyrus Dallin became an accomplished artist in painting as well as sculpture, befriending fellow artists such as Augustus Saint-Gaudens and John Singer Sargent.

Dallin created over 250 sculptures including figures of John Hancock, Oliver Wendell Holmes, and Sir Isaac Newton. Native American figures were a recurring theme. *Medicine Man* was the second of Dallin's Native American equestrian monuments. The first, called *Signal of Peace*, was exhibited at the Columbian Exposition in Chicago and permanently placed in Chicago's Lincoln Park. Cyrus later created *The Protest*, gold medal winner at the St. Louis Exposition in 1904, and *Appeal to the Great Spirit*, a monument that resides in front of the Museum of Fine Arts Boston. These equestrian monuments show Dallin's apprecization of the importance of the horse to the culture and viability of the Plains peoples.

Medicine Man rode many miles before settling in Fairmount Park. The sculpture won a gold medal at the Paris Exposition of 1900. Then it was on to the Pan-American Exposition in Buffalo before coming to our fair city where he has remained for over a century.

* * *

"While I have you here," Connie turns to address the *Medicine Man*, "I wonder if you might have some advice for me." Though his healing methods may be more out of date than his clothing, Connie is not given to let any potential expertise go untapped. She fires questions at him about everything from lumbar disc bulges to peroneal tendonitis.

Medicine Man looks down sadly, and says, "My medicine was not much help for my people who succumbed even more to the Europeans' diseases than to their bullets. European infections wiped out nine-tenths of my people. My only advice to you," he says earnestly, "is to get vaccinated and wear a mask. Now, be safe. And go in peace."

Sources:

Penny Balken Bach. *Public Art in Philadelphia*. Philadelphia,PA. Temple University Press, 1992

https://www.ncpedia.org/history/early/contact

https://www.medicinemangallery.com/cyrus-dallin-biography

Grey

YARN STRANDS

On Friday morning, Jewel craned her neck over her desktop monitor and told me that the 99 cent Store just donated all of their yarn to the Value Village over on Layton Avenue. Whole crates full, she said. I gave her a half-toothed smile as I scanned my badge and found my way to my cubicle.

On Saturday morning, I snaked through the aisles of Value Village—around a man with a fat belly, his three wily kids, and a misplaced cart—to get to the makeshift craft supply section. I was late. The store opened an hour ago. I had been thinking of knitting yarn since yesterday morning. Was the donated yarn hand-dyed? Probably not. Snowstorm grey, haystack yellow, potato sack brown—all colors I was hoping to find. I whizzed past the heavily used romance novels that crumbled at the seam, *Home and Country* magazines from ten years ago, and a short stack of those Dummies books from the 90s. Almost there. One marshmallow at a time, as my dad would say. "If you want to eat the whole bag, you'll have to start with one. There's no way around it." My dad's voice, grounded and easy, kept me in motion.

I'd have to get another plastic tote. Maybe they'd have one here, but Target is always a safe bet—plus the 15% off of storage bins was probably still running. Either way, there was no more room for knits of any sort: blankets, hats, scarfs—not even baby mittens. There's been at least ten accounts of rearranging, opening a tote, stuffing it past its capacity, and clasping the lid shut with force. I know my stock is out of control. Misty said she'd help research places to donate. Like a children's hospital or something. "Let's wait for Christmas," I told her. When she brought a bottle of red wine over last month, I made sure to shut the spare bedroom door. And now I can't bear to open it. Moving all the storage tubs in there broke a sweat. If I need my step ladder, I may just buy a new one because, like a fool, I left it in there. Seeing them stacked to the ceiling was too much. Rows and rows, placed like a perfect game of Tetris. Now, finished pieces lie rogue on my dining room table. They need a home out of view, especially since Misty drops in unannounced sometimes. *And* I need more yarn.

In the store, I turned the corner. All I had to do was get past the appliances and the old couches that I couldn't believe anyone would ever buy. But there he was. Bent over, where I could see the last of his grey tufts of hair, holding on with might. White hair frizzed out of his ears. His once white T-shirt was half way up his back, revealing the bones of his spine like a dinosaur. His Dickies drooped (he never wore a belt) and left your eyes sore from the long, visceral crack of his ass. *Every* time it was like walking in on your grandpa who had dementia. *Every* time, I felt a deep, empathetic pain for home nurses.

He was on the floor. The shelves behind him stood like giants, filled with tin and aluminum pieces of junk. His head was cranked fully on its side, as if he were having a secret conversation with whatever it was he hovered over. A sewing machine? There was whizzing and whining—a faint Hum Hum Hum. And just like that, I caught of glimpse of the mixing bowl. A stand mixer! He had attached the white, three-prong plug to the wall. The meticulous nature that had always been a part of him was somehow salvaged even when the dementia dropped down like a bomb. If he decided to haul that mixer to the register, he'd be sure to inquire with the cashier whether or not it worked and what the return policy was. And, of course, he had no need for this thing.

Just over his shaky frame I could see a red clump of yarn. Scratchy and scraggly. That's the stuff. I could smell the smell: a rainy day in a triangle-shaped attic. Off in the distance like a mirage, the yarn seemed to have good body to it—is that what a wine-o would say? Am I crazy? No. No, I'm not. I just know what I like in yarn—as I've told Misty anytime she questions my knitting "obsession." I threw my faux leather bag over my shoulder to make a run for it. I'd go back to the car to hide—buy some time. Surely, there were some yarn strands in the trunk I could pull out and knit with. Mitch could be occupied with that mixer for a while. But my bag, big and clumsy like me, hit a rack of shirts. A sign that read "T-shirts $2.99" clamored to the ground.

"Claire!"

I kept walking.

"Claire!" The sound of clashing metal exploded into the air.

I flinched and turned toward Mitch.

The mixer sat on the floor, abandoned. A beater lay stiff on the hard, thin tile. The cord was limp and lifeless. I knew he'd forget about that mixer forever.

His battered boat shoes—shoes this Value Village wouldn't accept as a donation—clunked toward me.

"Claire!"

"Hi, Mitch," I finally said.

"I knew you'd be here!" Mitch shouted.

With his embrace, I could feel his old loose skin fall onto me, asking for help. His bones knew. They wanted a rest. His smell crept into my clothes like a parasite. I'd throw them into the washer as soon as I got home. And even though it was mid-July, my nose became dry like it does in the depths of winter. The dryness stung my eyes, too. I knew what was coming. Paul. Mitch forgot a lot of things but never Paul. When I'm around Mitch, things unravel. I wanted to throw him to the side—smell yarn instead.

I unlatched his arms from my body.

"Mitch. It's good to see you," I said, looking into his hollow face.

"Claire!"

"Yeah, it's me."

"Let's get out of here."

"I don't know… I have a lot of errands to run today."

"No, no! We have to go!"

Both of his hands gripped my arm, begging me like a child. He nudged us to the door, nodding his head in that direction, but I secured my feet as best I could.

"Mitch, I can't."

"YES! Why aren't you there already?! He said he'd be with you."

The weight of my bag unsteadied my hold on the floor. A cashier looked over at us.

"C'mon. He won't be there much longer," Mitch said.

"Who?" I knew the mistake as soon as I said it.

"Who? Paul! Your dad! C'mon now."

We were walking. Mitch's one hand still on my wrist, pulling me.

The yarn. I didn't even get to inspect the new stock. I wanted to take a closer look at the red color—hold it in my hands. From where I was, it seemed like the kind of bright, silky red that darkens with time. The kind of red that stains a blue linen shirt with death—slashes, smears, and splatters of blood that could never be washed out, no matter the amount of OxiClean.

When the evergreens are full of snow, great big buckets of dumped white slosh, weighing down the boughs. When the bricks of the house sit neater, straighter, stiffer in the stark, crisp air. When the sky looks like a fog of grey, wrapping your place on Earth in a cold, vacuum-sealed bag. When the windows are laced in frost, smeared like old, cracked paint, and a cold billow of smoke escapes your warm inner self—that's when I see Paul.

Mitch was giddy; he scrambled us out of the single file doorway, running both of us into the wall like a toddler who hadn't grasped the art of walking yet. Out of the building, the sun was hot. The cicadas were singing in anguish. The heat beat through my veins, competing with my pulse. My heart-shaped sunglasses teased me at the bottom of my bag, but reaching them would require two hands.

"Call him."

"Who?" Fuck. The mistake again. It's difficult to keep straight: talking to a man whose lost his mind about a man who is no longer alive.

"Paul!"

Here we go.

"Oh, no, no, no. Let's just surprise him. He'll love to see you!"

I knew I should have kept my dad's phone line open a little while longer. Mitch could handle a voicemail, but a phone line that is no longer in service? Oh what Hell.

What did we look like? I always wondered that when I ran into Mitch, or rather when Mitch found me. Mitch was my dad's best man. Literally. At his wedding and in life. In his prime, Mitch was a firefighter. He came to all my birthday parties, bought me Legos, and even built princess castles with me. Paul and Mitch got drunk off Bacardi at my high school graduation party; Mitch fell into the pool—it was a hoot for everyone but their wives. One day, without warning, it was clear his memory was deteriorating. I was in college. My dad was always in denial. Sometimes, I feel like he let the car accident happen just so he didn't have to see his friend wither away. Now, out here on top of the black asphalt, he was withered. This wasn't Mitch. Mitch was muscular and tanned with a cigar in his mouth, ready to raise hell. Mitch Valetti. Italian from the outside in, but now he just looked *old*.

He smiled, a cracked frail little thing. "Okay, let's surprise him," he agreed.

I was guiding him now. Smooth sailing, I thought. And as soon as I thought it, I knew a slew of problems would rush in—tackle me like I had the football at the one yard line.

"Come on, Favre! What the fuck are you doing? You're the god damned best quarterback of the universe!" Their butts perched on the edge of the couch, mom harping from the kitchen to cut out the swearing, and my five-year-old self, dressed in a Brett Favre jersey, offered a bowl full of Cheeto Puffs to Mitch. He'd say, "Thank you, sweets" and kiss me on the cheek, smelling of beer and hotdog water.

We had almost crossed the long march of the asphalt jungle, my brow beginning to drip little salt droplets all the way down to my mouth. I licked my upper lip in satisfaction. The sidewalk was right there. The coffee shop not too much further. His apartment just about a mile beyond that. My mom and Tina, Mitch's wife, were both great at handling problems. It'd be nice if they were here. If Tina were still alive, Mitch wouldn't be living in an apartment. And if my mom Violet were still alive, she would have cooked my birthday dinner, leaving no reason for my dad to leave the house the night of the car crash. But they were all dead. Mitch might as well be. Was I dead, too?

"Paul!!" Mitch screamed.

I looked up from the careful stride of my tennis shoes that were keeping us on course.

Like a child who just spotted the ice cream truck, Mitch launched down the sidewalk, and it was then that I noticed his shoes didn't have any laces in them. One after the other, they flopped out from behind him, tossing themselves lightly into the air, revealing Mitch's even more pale and sockless feet.

Mitch saddled right into this man who was *not* my father. A stranger clad in flannel. Flannel in the summer—in this heat! My God, my dad wouldn't have ever worn flannel. He wore suit jackets and boat shorts, banana-patterned swim trunks, and T-shirts with bleach and paint stains. There were never flannel vests, flannel long-sleeved shirts, or flannel pajama pants—not even for my mom's annual Christmas photo.

"Paul!" Mitch called again, his hand reached for the man's shoulder.

"Mitch!" I yelled after him. I was behind him now, partially out of breath, partially stunned.

"Whoa, buddy—" The stranger's arms were up in the air with his palms outward. His eyes darted at me flippantly.

"Paul. Wow! Paul. We were—we were just coming to see you!"

"Come on now. Uh. I'm not Paul." His hand carefully tried to remove Mitch's arms from his space.

Then, in what seemed like an odd delay of reflexes, the woman on non-Paul's side screamed. Her screechy scream transformed my mood into irritation. I actually rolled my eyes, but things were moving quick. Mitch bumped his chest into this man's shoulder and tried to whap him on the butt. The energy seemed to manifest from some deep place within.

"Earl! Earl!" The hysterical woman kept up. The more she bellowed her shriek into the stale, suffocating air, the more baffled I became. What was her deal? Get a grip, I wanted to shout.

But it was too late. I saw the change in the man's movements. His intentions were not aligned for Mitch's state of mind. He gathered his arms close to his body, and with one sharp shove, Mitch was on the ground.

"What the fuck is wrong with you?" I threw my purse and leapt to Mitch on the sidewalk. His butt landed in the crunchy grass while his legs lay flaccid on the sidewalk.

"I'm calling 911!" The woman announced, reaching for her phone.

"Were you just going to keep standing there when your grandpa was humping me?!" The man chimed in.

I could feel the man's aggression building. I just kept stroking Mitch's wrist, holding it limp in my lap. "Mitch. Mitch. Can you hear me? Are you okay?"

He didn't look like a man who had just been knocked to the ground. He looked calm—sort of like Snow White in the kiss-awaiting casket scene. And just like Snow, Mitch wasn't dead. I almost felt bad disturbing him. Was he dreaming of hanging out with his best bud, playing pool and throwing back shots of Jameson? It was nice, too, ya know? He hadn't been this quiet all day. And then, it hit me again: yarn. Ball after ball of yarn. I probably wouldn't get the chance to knit at all today now.

"My husband's been attacked!"

"Can you shut her up?" I said, standing up again.

This guy was brushing off his sleeves as if recovering from a fighting match. Glancing up and down the sidewalk, there was not a breathing body in sight. I looked at this dumb asshole up and down, swiped my knees clean from some grass that stuck, and then I wailed after him. My sort of run attack worked well enough as I jumped, grabbed at his clavicle, and pounced him to the ground. But that was the extent of my fighting ability. It didn't matter that I was a woman. His manly aggression came at me full force—that sort of unkempt, abandoned anger that dwells in the bottom of men. There were no shouts or words to be had; he had me below him in under a second, and before my eyes closed for a while, the side of my head felt the reign of his fist: arduous and unjustified.

My head was rushing. Hot and pounding. Mitch? I tried to open my eyes but they didn't want to move.

"Mitch?" I squeaked.

No reply.

My back was damp with perspiration, and I could feel the sun's glare through my eyelids. Even the needles of grass seemed slightly soggier beneath my body.

"Mitch..." I tried to be louder. Still, no reply.

I sat up in one swing. Pain drilled down my spinal cord. Only my right eye would open, and panic sunk into my chest. Too chicken to feel around my eye socket, I looked toward Mitch. I saw his body heave up and down slowly, so I let out a sigh. Okay, one marshmallow at a time.

"Hey! Mitch!"

"What's with all the racket, honey? I'm trying to get in a little cat's nap before dinner."

"Huh?"

"Annie, quiet now! Papa is resting."

Shit. The good news: my dead dad Paul was off the hook. The worst news: I had been reimagined as Mitch's daughter Annie. That was the only Annie I knew. She was older than I. When I was five, she must've been old enough to drive. I don't remember her much, but I never got the impression that she took any special liking toward me.

I suddenly missed *my* father.

"What about Paul?"

"Annie, stop talking nonsense. Go practice your tuba and leave Daddy alone."

"God damn it!" I screamed. This was not one marshmallow. This was the whole fucking bag. I clenched my eyes closed and grinded my teeth at the resulting pain. Tears made their way out, stinging and hot.

I'd have to call Annie. What else could I do? There was no way Mitch could go home alone, even if I was able to get him there safely. Maybe I still had Annie's number saved. I scanned around the ground for my purse. My bag looked like a casualty of sorts. My sunglasses were stepped on with small bits of plastic around the frame. Other purse jumble littered the scene nearby: a bamboo knitting needle, a Sharpie, and a loose business card of some sort. In the mess, I also spotted the shattered screen of my cell phone.

I could tell from here that its life had been depleted for good. Whole glass chunks were sticking out of it. My brain was moving too fast. The last text from Dad. He called me Claire Bell, right? Something about drive safely— even though he never made it safely to my birthday dinner. Did he say I love you? Could I get that text back from the Cloud? I could ask Misty. Did I take a screenshot of the text thread? Would it be on my laptop?

Without notice, my body convulsed, and I puked into the grass. I coughed. Then, I screamed.

"C'mon now! I'm going to get your mother on the phone if you keep this up."

She was dead. Tina. Annie's mother. I had to think.

"Dad! I'm sorry, but I need to call mom. Can I use your cell? Then I'll be quiet. Promise."

"It's in the kitchen. Now scram!"

"No, no, Dad. It's not; I looked. I swear. I think it's in your pocket. If I could just call mom, you can go back to sleep."

The sound of soft wheels hitting the uneven sidewalk squares hit my ears. I looked up and saw thick, square-shaped black sunglasses: a mom and a stroller. It was bright as hell, and this woman was already pulling off her shades to get a clearer shot at the scene in front of her. She was squinting, assessing us—almost in speaking distance now.

"Are you two okay?" I couldn't pull my eyes from her tightly wrapped bun that sat on the top of her skull like a bird—like a ball of yarn.

"Oh, yeah. My grandpa just fell. He's okay. Just slow moving."

She stopped, and I resisted the urge to lightly touch my swollen eye. Not a sound arose from the stroller. She looked back and forth between Mitch and me. "Do you need some help?"

"Grandpa?!" Mitch shouted.

"No, we'll be okay. Thank you, though."

"Your lip is bleeding." The woman placed her sunglasses atop her head and pointed at my face.

I drew a finger to my bottom lip, and sucked it, tasting the bitterness. Should I undo the lie? Start from the beginning and spill all these confusing truths out to this woman who I didn't know if I could trust.

"Annie. Here! Take my phone and keep your promise now!"

"I'm just going to call my cousin Annie for help; she lives right up the road."

She looked at me hard. "Is your name Annie?"

"Yeah," I laughed. "First cousins having the same first name. It's a joy." More lies. They were stacking, stumbling like the end of a Jenga game. And I was sure this was the end. My insides throbbed for release. What would she do if she figured it out? I hadn't done anything wrong.

A loud, obtrusive cry protruded from the stroller. And then a steady wailing followed. My shoulders relaxed, and I wiped sweat from my hairline.

"Would you like me to wait here with you?" She was now sliding the stroller wheels up and down the sidewalk gingerly. "Shhh, shhh. It's okay," she said to the baby.

"No, really, we're good."

"Okay. Well take care and be well."

"Thanks, you too!"

Carefully, I watched her disappear down the sidewalk. I didn't move my head—in case she was also watching me. But I knew she wouldn't come back. Maybe she could've helped. When my dad was dead, I was one of the last people on the scene. The ambulance finally pulled away, and I found my arm outstretched, wondering what his hand felt like in mine—the memory already gone. In the hospital, his hands never felt like my dad's.

I folded my knees up into my chest and clung to them like how I'd clutch brand-new yarn balls up close to my face, smelling in the old. I was out of yarn. I was out of ideas. It must be near two in the afternoon. As the heat beat down on my open chest, a thin layer of sweat wrapped itself around my breasts. I looked at Mitch. He didn't seem bothered by the warmth, but he must be feeling it. Even in his more solid days, he'd never been one to complain. Except, I suppose, when Annie interrupted his naps. My childhood memories are overabundant with Mitch at our house. I never really knew what his own family dynamic looked like. Where did Annie's grief with me spur from?

Annie really was my only option here.

"C'mon, Dad. We're going inside." I stood up, and walked over to Mitch, reaching out a hand for him to follow suit.

"Honey, quit your hollerin'!"

At least we were on the same storyline. I'm still Annie. Mitch is still my dad.

"It's too hot. Let's get to a shady area. Then, you can rest again."

"I suppose it's a bit warm."

"Yeah, it is. We just got to go a little over that way. C'mon. Give me your hand, and I'll help you up."

"I don't think so."

"Fuck you, Mitch!" I regretted the words as soon as they spewed out. Did Paul have to deal with this bullshit, too? How did he do it?

Looking at him on the ground was like looking at a lump of discarded yardwork scraps. Mitch was covered in grass, collaged with sticks, and smeared with dirt. I wasn't sure how I'd manage his fragility. He *did* reach out his hand though, and with the best squat I could muster, I hoisted his body up, outstretching like an accordion that hadn't been moved in years. He almost took another tumble, but he made it up, and I wrapped my arm around his waist. The smell was unpleasant, but his underarm odor was familiar. And that was pleasant.

"Where are we going?"

"Right over there by that building." I pointed at Value Village with his industrial size flip phone in my free hand.

"But Paul's at the coffee shop. We have to go that way!" He tried twisting his body around, plummeting my balance from the shock of his movements and memory jumps.

"Uh, I left my phone in the store though. We just have to go back really quick."

"Claire?"

"Uh, yeah, Mitch?"

"Where's Annie? Wasn't she just with us?"

"We have to call her!"

"Oh, okay. Well let's get this gig a kickin'. The coffee's getting stale."

"Well, let's start walking then!"

The walk across the parking lot was mostly quiet. A few hums came from Mitch every so often, but it was still just as hot. A heavy dose of adrenaline still raced its way through my limbs, but I knew I'd feel like shit in the morning. How long had I been out? Had that dickface really touched me? Do I report him? I tried to scratch those thoughts out for now; Annie was causing serious anxiety. My palms were clammy. I could hear her—the condescending attitudes and the preachy rhythmic flow of her voice. There was no other way to put it; she was a bitch.

The bench outside of the store was available and shady. I didn't even have to tell Mitch to take a seat. He was tired. A small smile cracked my lip open. Now, the yarn did seem a bit silly. I didn't need more of it so soon, really. I could have stayed home instead, found a way to work with the scraps. I could call Misty, but I couldn't tell her where I was. She would know. It would be the finale. The last I'd knit. I could see her: parking her little Subaru Outback on the road outside my house, walking with pleasure up to my front door, and without knocking, announcing her presence and reason for intrusion—"Where are the bins?! We're donating them today. Let's go." She'd probably have me call the therapist on her phone—the number would be queued up. Tearing apart my bins of completed knitting projects, she'd hold up a mitten, and scream in outrage, "This does not spark joy! We're getting rid of it!"

I don't know where the knitting came from. I'd never done it before. Maybe it was the idea that I wanted to make a hat for someone in the same hospital as my dad. A cancer patient? Maybe my dad told me about how granny used to knit him little yellow sweaters when he was a kid. It's hard to separate the truths. But the day I came home from his funeral, I found some yarn in a box of run down arts and craft supplies, and looked up a YouTube video, and I had my first misshapen hat. Now, there were hundreds of hats.

I looked down at the enlarged block numbers of the senior edition cell phone in my hand. My eyes were heavy. I couldn't visually make out the numbers through the tears, but I knew her number by heart. Please answer, please answer, please answer.

"Hello?"

"I need help," I said.

"Claire?"

"Yes. I'm by Value Village."

"Enough. I'm coming. I'll be there in five."

Author's Note

I saw this man—Mitch—at an actual resale shop near my house, and the way his eyes talked to the nonworking appliances sparked character development instantly. But the story goes beyond Mitch. Writing about Mitch and Claire has helped me handle my own abandoned relationships and figure out what's truly important in life.

Shaun Bailey

CASH FOR KEYS

It wasn't the first bomb to wash ashore in Bay Point, but it would be the last. These ... "unexploded ordinances," they could blow at any moment, or so a seaman once told him—and he would know. It was with this in mind that Lawrence bent over, bear hugged the World War II bombshell, and wrestled it from the beach. Its service to America was not yet over.

Lawrence leaned back as he carried the rusty hulk atop his ample belly. The bomb's weight caused him to shuffle more than stride, sandals and all. This was so much the case that his Morey's Pier t-shirt was soon speckled with sweat. Lawrence was quite the sight; at least, he would've been had anyone been there to see him. Instead, he made his way past the town's long row of empty cottages, each one abandoned by order of the state's Department of Environmental Protection.

But not his place ... not until 5 p.m. anyway.

It took Lawrence more than an hour to manhandle the bullet-shaped shell onto Bay Point's only road. To reach it he had to walk the long way around a cinderblock sea wall, or what was left of it. This ramp-like edifice was now collapsing into Delaware Bay, and that which remained sat covered in slippery green algae. This wavy ribbon of concrete was enough to make any stonemason shake his head, yet it endured, a monument to government incompetence.

At least he had good company. To his left, gulls called from the homes' disintegrating docks, as if to ask after those who'd fled. To his right, cicadas buzzed in waves that rose and fell, like the cool breezes that made the town so appealing. Meanwhile, red-winged blackbirds watched from their perches atop vibrant green stems of waist-high cordgrass. Lawrence surveyed them all as he stopped for breaks, but he couldn't help himself. His mind inevitably wandered, contemplating the fates of his former neighbors. But then he caught himself, remembering his date with the state.

One o'clock. Better get moving.

Jane gazed at the Tea Burners' Monument from a bench in the Old Market Place. Normally she ate inside Aunt Betty's Kitchen, but not today. Today she ventured outdoors to enjoy her oyster po' boy. It was her first chance to soak up some spring sunshine after all, and she had to act fast. The breeze wouldn't keep the greenflies at bay for long. Besides, she needed the solitude. It wasn't every day she offered cash for keys.

Jane enjoyed a few bites and then began to prepare, first by reviewing paperwork the state had sent by certified mail ... thick contracts written in legalese. One by one, she confirmed each homeowner had accepted the state's terms: to sell their storm-ravaged homes for Bay Point's demolition. In all there must have been three dozen contracts spanning four years. And those contracts had company: Seabreeze, Money Island, Dyer's Cove ... ghost towns, save for some holdouts. Jane had inked so many contracts that she could barely fit them in her briefcase. The only way she could keep them organized was to wrap thick rubber bands around each bundle, which she kept in alphabetic order. With that accomplished, she stared down at the top settlement, its blue signature scribbled across the page as if a high tide had swamped the signer's feet, never mind nor'easters and hurricanes.

Jane reminisced about those homeowners until she snapped to, slapped a blank contract atop the pile, and peeked inside her purse. There she saw what brokers called "The great negotiator": $2,000 in cash. The only question was, Would Lawrence Fitzgerald accept it? Would he surrender his home to the state, or would it be the waves that claimed eminent domain?

Lawrence's house soon came into view, scars and all. Chief among its flaws were missing strips of powder-blue siding, which had long since gone the way of Hurricane Sandy's storm surge. It wasn't a good look. The superstorm's swells had exposed the shack's plywood underbody, which now appeared grayish brown, knotted and dotted with half-hammered nails. But that wasn't the worst indignity; not by far. On the door, written in bright-orange spray paint, was the letter "C", as in condemned. A building inspector had driven all the way from Trenton just to emblazon that mark on his home; on every home. Below that was duct tape where flyers had once hung, each one listing phone numbers, meeting dates, and deadlines; today's in fact, in large bold type. Lawrence had torn these down of course. He burned them, but what really burned was the humiliation of their neon brand. His home deserved better.

Lawrence peered through mop-topped stalks of Phragmites at the levee that was Bay Point Road. True to form, its only traveler was a terrapin turtle retreating to the salt marsh. Otherwise, no outsiders approached, and so he wrestled his keepsake onward. Along the way Lawrence ignored that which reminded him of his former neighbors, but then he saw Sammy's cottage. Its stack of traps evoked memories of picking blue crabs into the early morning, until Sammy would finally throw in the towel; not for lack of hunger, or crabs, mind you. Inevitably they ran out of beer.

Next door lay Hank's rusty oyster dredge. "I'll be back for it," he said in parting. "Don't let nobody steal it." But that was a year ago. Now knee-high weeds had all but hidden it from view. Yet there it was, the rig affectionately known as Allstate. Hank had dubbed it that in jest of course, but the name stuck given the many oyster eats it had stocked, almost all of them fundraisers. After all, that dredge was the village's best insurance policy; a real lifesaver when someone's septic tank failed, they needed surgery, or, heaven forbid, a headstone. But there was no oyster eat big enough to save Bay Point.

Lawrence had nearly made it past Hank's house when an enormous C-130 aircraft buzzed the coastline. The green and grey behemoth was merely flying maneuvers, just as it did every week, yet Lawrence ditched his discovery all the same. The transport plane then banked over the bay and pointed its four turboprops directly at Lawrence, causing him to crouch behind the thin boughs of a loblolly pine. At any moment he expected to see muzzle flashes, perhaps bombs falling from bay doors. Baileytown was just a dozen miles away after all, its craters still visible from many a target practice during World War II. Was Bay Point now doomed to the same fate?

The pilots crossed Bay Point's narrow road and then jerked the yoke back, causing the C-130 to gain altitude. As it climbed, the plane's roaring sound gradually receded into the uplands, in the direction of McGuire Air Force Base. In time, Lawrence eased out from his hiding spot and muttered, "Maneuvers ... that's all it is." Even so, he scanned the horizon for more planes, more eyes in the sky. When the only spies he saw were red-tailed hawks, he cautiously resumed his march, though not without straining his back.

The road's sand grated at Lawrence's feet, yet it was Cedar Creek that commanded his attention. The tide was pushing in its turbid water, swamping muddy banks crawling with crabs, turtles, and wading birds. Between he and these flats sat his duck blind, which looked no worse for wear than the day he built it. Whereas winds had carried off shingles from nearby homes, the opposite was true of his blind. The reeds making up its thatch roof were still neatly fastened in place. High waves had knocked several structures off their concrete foundations, yet the blind's pilings looked immovable in the face of swift water. Even the grasses masking its facade were still stapled in place, for the most part. The same could not be said for locals' shrubbery. Salt water had poisoned most of it, and the state's neglect had finished off the rest.

Lawrence's house had just come into view when he took leave of his burden for the sake of his bladder. Standing there by the roadside, he looked over his truck and trailer piled high with belongings. His attention then wandered to Bay Point Road and, for a final time, he admired his work. The town's lone electric line no longer dangled from utility poles, flapping in the breeze; on the contrary, his skills as a commercial electrician allowed him to reconnect its broken links—no thanks to the power company. Now the line ran from pole to pole and, eventually, all the way north to Cedarville, some five miles away ... not that it mattered; no one had stayed. Even so, Lawrence's eyes followed the line inland. That's when a glint of sun revealed a white Cadillac approaching the outpost.

Lawrence collected himself and looked about before dragging the shell behind a derelict boat. He emerged swiping at the mud, rust, and dust now soiling his shirt and blue jeans. He wiped himself clean as best he could, though traces remained that might never disappear, like a pylon in the water, a foundation in the grass ... like Bay Point.

Jane gripped the steering wheel as she slowed to 15 miles per hour. The tide was in so far that its waters now lapped at the asphalt, where guard rails should be but weren't. In some places it had even topped Bay Point Road, its smooth surface reflecting white clouds above. The sedan's tires splashed through this water, making nearby birds flee in great flocks, yet it was Jane who seemed spooked. She leaned forward, white knuckled, and veered over the road's center line.

If only she had checked the tide chart.

Jane craned her neck to better see the town's first house and its three-story observation deck. It was the sort of tower one might expect to find in a national forest, atop a mountain, only the builders capped it with a home-made lantern room complete with a cupola, catwalk, and flagpole. A sign in the window read "Bank Owned" in large red letters. Another sign read "No Trespassing", though it was clearly unsafe to enter. Recent storms had ripped away most of the home's deck boards ... balusters too. Those that remained had been battered askew; this, despite their six-foot elevation above the bay.

The neighboring house wasn't there at all. The only thing left was a wooden stairway leading to what had once been its dock. To be safe though, someone had blocked its first step by nailing a board between its newel posts. A short distance away sat the dock's stainless steel utility sink. Waves slapped at its basin like a kitten with its toy, as if in payback for all the fish it had been accessory to scaling. It looked to be a new sink too, despite a few barnacles. Not one dent, yet no one was coming for it. Instead, it swayed back and forth as waves washed against the rubble in which it was lodged.

Other houses had nary a scratch. Jane peered at one such home sporting a new roof, air conditioner, awnings, picnic table and patio. Off the side, brightly-colored toys poked through the surface of a children's sandbox, and a baby swing swayed crooked in the breeze. It looked as if she could list and sell the home within a month—two tops. Yet bulldozers would soon arrive on great flat-bed trailers to ensure that no one would ever call this place home again.

Jane stared at the baby swing until she noticed the pictures children had painted on its neighboring fence. There was a blue bird, red octopus, green turtle, brown mice, and orange stars, each one arranged as if to tell a story, like an ancient pictograph. Then she noticed how the fence made up one side of a low tree fort, and this evoked a smile as she looked back to the roadway. There a man stood with his hands on his hips, causing Jane to gasp, jerk the wheel, and mash her foot atop the brake. When she looked up, her car had stopped just inches from the unflinching figure, his feet spanning the center line.

Jane leaned out her open window while adjusting her sunglasses, which had slipped to the end of her narrow nose.

"I am so sorry, Mr. Fitzgerald. I didn't see you there," she explained. "You appeared just like—"

"A ghost ... in a ghost town? Come on, Jane. Let's get this over with."

Jane parked her car where it had abruptly stopped: in the middle of the roadway. There she used the rearview mirror to primp her appearance, after which she grunted while retrieving her briefcase, which had fallen onto the littered floorboard. Jane struggled to clutch this bag to her chest while shutting the car door. Finally, with a raised eyebrow and a curled lip, she followed Lawrence as he led her to a nearby picnic table. She didn't sit at first though. Instead she pulled a silk handkerchief from her jacket, which she used to dust paint chips from her bench seat. Only when this was clean did she finally sit and position her briefcase. Lawrence, meanwhile, waited patiently while watching dolphins swim parallel to shore.

"Everything's packed, but I'll be damned if I'm leaving for less than we agreed," Lawrence began.

Jane opened her briefcase by releasing its two locks with a metallic *click*. From it she pulled a contract from off a stack, its stretched rubber band twanging like a guitar string. She placed this form in front of Lawrence and, on top of it, she placed a smooth stone, to prevent the bay's breeze from snatching it away.

"If you direct your eyes to the bottom of Page 2," Jane began, "you'll be happy to see the sum we discussed: $2,000. The preceding language states that you will vacate the premises by 5 p.m. today; empty it of all your belongings, appliances, and pets; leave all copper piping to prevent gas leaks; surrender your keys to the state's hired representative ... that's me; depart in a polite and prompt manner; and, most importantly, abstain from future lawsuits. The third page details how you're now free from having to repay the balance of your mortgage.

"Lastly, you'll see your signature there at the very end, but not mine," Jane said, moving the paperweight to reveal a scribbled name. "Can we both agree that's your signature, Lawrence?"

"Yes, that's my signature," he sighed.

Above them, Lawrence saw a trio of seagulls scavenging for what history had taught them was a picnic lunch. Every now and then one swooped low, braked by flapping its wings, and then retreated to the heavens screeching its reconnaissance. The thought of such meals made Lawrence look to his cooler in need of ice, beside which his patio umbrella poked out from the pile. But then the gulls recaptured his attention and so he reveled in their sound.

"Stupid dump chickens," Jane muttered, swatting at flies. "I have also yet to sign this check. It contains the fair market value of your home's equity. Subtracting for the home equity loan you withdrew for repairs, its total comes to $35,000; but, obviously there's more. To make your decision easier," Jane continued, pulling a stack of twenties from her purse, "the state has authorized me to pay you $2,000 in cash, but in exchange you must surrender your keys—without incident. Do we have a deal?"

Jane looked up to gauge her statement's impact on Lawrence. His attention, however, was focused on the birds.

"Mr. Fitzgerald?" she asked.

Lawrence lowered his eyes and cocked his head, his hands folded before him.

"As the state's representative, I am now obligated to walk the property before signing your check. This ensures the state is spending taxpayers' money responsibly through its buyout program.

"May I have the key?"

"Yes, of course," Lawrence said. He reached into his pocket and retrieved his key ring, which jingled as he pulled it free. He picked past the bundle's bottle opener and pen knife to locate his house key. It hadn't left his keychain in more than 20 years, so its small metal ring was unforgiving. Even so, he pried it open using his short, dirt-laden fingernails, slid off the key and held it high with a smile, at which point Jane plucked it from his fingertips. Key in hand, she turned on her heels and marched up the front walk, clipboard at the ready.

With Jane occupied, Lawrence slinked away and jogged back to the boat, but this time he used a new technique to carry his keepsake: He heaved the shell onto his shoulder using both hands, as if it was a log. This method worked better, as he now walked twice as fast as before. Soon Lawrence had the relic beside his trailer and, having no plan, he placed it inside his cooler, where he padded it with popsicles and TV dinners.

Lawrence was catching his breath when a seagull screeched as if to comment on his folly. He glared at the scavenger perched atop his trailer, its white droppings streaking down the fender. "You know, if you were smart, you'd have saved that for the Caddy over yonder," he said with a nod of his head. Then he walked to the beach so as to revel in the town's final moments. There Lawrence stood among the weathered pilings of his friends' docks and decks, each of them in speckled with barnacles. Nearby, several horseshoe crabs struggled to escape a collapsed foundation's broken blocks, their spider-like legs searching for sand. This sight compelled Lawrence to render aid. He returned each creature to the sea, but, to his surprise, the ungrateful crabs turned their backs on the bay. Instead they obeyed their instincts by returning to the beach ingrained in their DNA, even if it meant certain doom.

Lawrence looked from the birds to the barnacles to the crabs. Then with a sigh he said, "You'll have this place all to yourselves soon enough."

Jane opened a window and yelled, "I thought we discussed 'broom clean!'"

Lawrence smiled for a moment, but then his expression sobered. "You reckon they swept Atlantis too?" he asked.

Jane narrowed her eyes and pursed her lips. Finally she waved for him to come inside, closed the window and, for some reason, locked it. Even so, Lawrence lingered there for a moment listening for curse words, but he couldn't hear any; at least, not over the surf, so he walked uphill along the house's west side. There he searched for anything he might have left in the sparse dune grass that remained, but all he found was a life ring so weathered it was no longer seaworthy.

At the road he walked past Jane's car, but he slowed as he noticed the back seat's pillow and blankets. In the floorboard sat a hot plate plugged into a cigarette lighter, and a miniature coffee maker leaned against it, complete with a dreg of coffee in its pot. Up front a pink carry-on suitcase rode shotgun, clothes poking out from its unzipped top. Its matching cosmetic bag sat atop the center console, dried toothpaste dotting its side.

Back at the picnic table, Jane opened her briefcase and retrieved the check she had promised Lawrence. While searching for her pen she asked, "Any other keys you know of?"

"No, ma'am."

"In that case, here's your buyout," Jane said, signing the check. She then reached into her purse and retrieved the state's cash incentive.

Lawrence's calloused hand snatched both the check and cash. Once his, he quickly confirmed their value before tucking them in the back pocket of his blue jeans. Lawrence then rose from the table and began to leave when he stopped and, looking at the ground, asked, "You been living in your car, Jane?"

After a moment's pause, Jane took a deep breath and said, "That hurricane hit a lot more than this backwater. Rest of us got to get by too."

Lawrence lingered while looking north at Bay Point Road. Then he looked east, where Paris Road ended at the creek. All the while he used his hand to shield his eyes from the sun, as if honoring Bay Point with a final salute.

"Well, you've got my key, but Dalton's place, down there at the very end; it's also unlocked. Still got a bed inside too. You pull your car real close to the far side there and, hell—won't no one know you're there ... not till the bulldozers come anyhow."

"And what about you, Lawrence? You'll know I'm there."

"Hell, I ain't got no beef with you, Jane. Now the State of New Jersey? FEMA? Yes, ma'am. I aim to have a word with them—and you should too, but us? Shoot, this'll be the last you see of me ... probably ever."

Jane placed Lawrence's contract neatly atop her pile, wrapped a thick rubber band around it, and then returned the stack to her briefcase. There it sat atop other piles, each donning the name of another village.

"So where will you go from here, Lawrence?"

He smiled for only the second time that afternoon and replied, "You needn't worry about me, Jane. I got it all figured out."

Jane waited until Lawrence was looking. Then she shut her briefcase and locked it by turning its combination dials. Exhaling a deep sigh, she then rose from the picnic table and extended her hand, which Lawrence shook with a firm grip.

"Thanks for not pulling any stunts," Jane said. "You wouldn't believe what some people try, even when no one else will help them. I wish you nothing but the best."

Lawrence nodded and then walked to his truck and trailer. Along the way a cool breeze wafted through his thinning hair, causing him to look back at his former home, where he would never again watch another sun set across Delaware Bay. This thought prompted Lawrence to snatch a shovel from his trailer and rub some sand on its short handle, like a baseball bat. He then cursed aloud, tested his grip and marched back, in the direction of Jane's car.

"Lawrence—one more thing," Jane shouted from the window. "A state trooper's up the way watching to make sure you leave peacefully! That's not my call! The state does it for everyone!"

Jane paused to wave with a big smile, then continued, "Just thought I'd mention it so you don't get in any trouble!"

Lawrence didn't wave back. Instead he returned to his pickup and heaved the shovel back among his belongings. This brought him within reach of his cooler, which Lawrence opened just a crack. Glancing at his watch, he then slammed the cooler shut and stepped onto the truck's running board, where he opened a rusty door. Its disintegrating hinges groaned in protest. Rather than reminisce, Lawrence simply dropped onto his seat, tilted the mirror toward his former house, and started the engine. A few minutes later he spotted the highway patrolman parked beneath the sign marking Jones Island Road. Behind him a line of laborers worked the Garden State's final farm before it sloped off into the sea. Again, he didn't wave.

Lawrence drove through Cedarville, over the Cohansey River at Fairton, and into the city of Bridgeton. Once there he loaded up on groceries, especially non-perishables. Then he headed south again, toward Greenwich, but he took his time. Doing so allowed him to leave his military antique on the historical society's doorstep once it had closed. Then he tore out of there, his trailer rattling and hopping curbs along the way.

Jane ventured down the road to the former Dalton home, just as Lawrence suggested. Not only was its door unlocked, but also she found that it still had hot running water. This discovery sent her running for her towel, toiletries, and robe. Jane smiled as she carried these through the living room, where the descending sun beamed through a picture window; its width so wide it nearly spanned the room.

The sunset's warm rays glinted off something as Jane rushed by, so she slowed and then stopped to look closer. In the front room, she found wires leading beneath the door to a built-in bench. This sight caused her to cock her head, step forward, and flip up the seat's floral-print cushion. Connected to the wires was a corroded hunk of cylindrical metal; something she had never seen before. Jane then followed the wires outside, where the waves' spray had wet the decking. There she stepped forward and peered through the dusk's golden glow. This light illuminated even more wires trailing from one house to the next, all the way up the town's long row of empty cottages. Jane blinked her eyes tight, as if to correct her vision and, slowly, her mouth fell open.

The trailer rocked as Lawrence crossed the pock-marked parking lot of Hancock Harbor Marina. He could see its load shifting in the rearview mirror, so he slowed his truck to a crawl atop the lot's crushed oyster-shell surface. Eventually he parked along the water's edge, pulled on a sweat jacket, and set off for the Bait Box Restaurant. He had only made it a few feet when an unseen voice said, "The light's out on your trailer you know."

Lawrence turned to see a slender man wiping oil from his hands atop the bow of a docked sailboat. He wore navy blue coveralls and a Phillies cap turned backward. A stubby cigar sat deep in the corner of his mouth; so deep it looked as though it may singe his face at any moment.

Lawrence sauntered forward so as to better see the man and replied, "Well, sir, I ain't traveling too far. In fact I aim to strike a trade: the whole lot for a boat—truck included. Anyone you know may be interested in such a swap?"

The mechanic appraised the offer but didn't move from where he stood. All the while he rubbed the blackened rag across his hands, his body swaying with each wave rippling ashore. His squinted eyes moved back and forth from Lawrence to the overloaded trailer and, rather than question why, he said, "Well I hope you don't got your heart set on no yacht."

"No, no ... I was thinking a sloop, or a cutter; nothing so big I can't manage it myself."

"And everything there's included?"

"Yes, sir," Lawrence returned, "everything but the essentials: my clothes, tools, food ... my fishing gear I suppose."

The mechanic craned his neck and leaned from side to side. He surveyed the trailer's appliances and furniture, much of which looked older than their seller. He then peered at the pickup's cracked windshield, dented fender, and missing tailgate; its sagging muffler and rusted-out doors. After a long pause he shook his head, removed his cigar and considered his response. Finally he sighed and said, "Sorry, friend. Your rig there, it just ain't worth that much. Maybe someone inside can help you."

Lawrence looked back at his truck laden with his possessions. Then he reached into his pocket and pulled from it his state buyout. He raised the check in one hand and his cash in the other, as if surrendering to the police. Then he continued, "Well I suppose there's this too."

"Well then," the mechanic said, smiling in spite of his cigar, "let's take us a lap round the marina."

Jane had just alerted the police when she saw her broker's Mercedes pull up outside the Dalton house. He carried a thick roll of blueprints as he approached wearing a navy blue suit, brown oxfords, and sunglasses. The man didn't bother to knock, but instead burst in and announced, "I have some big news, Jane, and I think it will cheer you up. Follow me here ..."

"Steve, you don't understand. The police—"

"The police will have their own precinct right here in Bay Point. What I want to discuss is *your* house, Jane. Look here," Steve said, unrolling his blueprints. "None of this would be possible without you, so we have reserved— right here, look—your beautiful new home with sweeping views of both the bay and golf course. It's just a short walk from the clubhouse too."

"Steve, Lawrence Fitzpatrick—he wired—"

"What he does with his buyout is his business, Jane. And you needn't worry about his fate. Every *new* home will be elevated high above storm surge levels; their windows will have hurricane-proof, rolling-steel shutters. Reinforced dunes will span the entire shoreline under our feet. And the best part? The best part is how the state is subsidizing it all; even paying us to—"

"Steve—would you just look?" Jane shouted.

The broker straightened his posture, blinked his eyes and replied, "Hell, Jane, what could be more important than this?" Then he looked out the window to see a white sloop traversing the shore, sails down. Unimpressed, he looked at Jane and scoffed, "Hardly the yacht that'll dock here someday."

"No—look!" she said, pointing to the mess of metal and wires hidden inside the bench.

Steve's brow furrowed as he peered out the window, toward the sailboat. That's when he noticed a thin line of bubby water traveling landward, in the house's direction. He watched as it moved closer, quickly traveling from the boat to shore as if it was a dolphin's fin rippling the water just below its surface. It wasn't until the final stretch that Steve finally saw smoke emanating from the long, waterproof fuse cutting across the beach.

Only then did he drop his plans.

Author's Note:

"Cash for Keys" is a reflection on my 12 years working in New Jersey's southern bayshore communities. This region is where the State of New Jersey is buying and demolishing homes owned by the working poor to make way for higher seas and stronger storms. Meanwhile, the state and federal governments have invested billions to protect wealthy property owners along the popular Atlantic Coast. These decisions will be debated for generations, and these debates will fuel great art. "Cash for Keys" is intended to spark that art's creation, and fuel further debate.

Adam Matson

MAYONAISE

Melissa stood at the kitchen counter, making a sandwich. Her phone chimed with a text message from Allison: "Chris Ritter committed suicide." For some reason, the first thing she thought of was Chris' old joke about the Smashing Pumpkins' song, "Mayonaise."

She finished building her sandwich, and now the components, including a mayonnaise jar, sat on the counter, waiting to be replaced. Melissa just stood there, wondering if she was still hungry.

Alone in the house, she sat down at the kitchen table, stared outside at the withering late-February snow. It seemed like the snow had been deeper when she was a kid. Like there had been more of it. Like whole epochs of her young life had taken place in Maine winters. She thought of Chris Ritter, when they were on the ski team in junior high, his practical approach to negotiating a slalom course: "First rule: don't die."

She decided to call Allison, rather than reply by text. She had not seen Chris Ritter in more than fifteen years- nor Allison in five, she realized. One of the gloomy facts of adulthood was that many old friends drifted away.

Allison told her that Chris had died in Antarctica, where he had been studying ice melt. Melissa had read Chris' various published articles on climate change. Chris studied the deep snow of the past, looking for microbes, remnants of past life, clues to what kind of future the melt might reveal. The tone of his articles had progressed over the years, like stages of cancer, from informative, to alarmist, to grave.

"There was a note," Allison said, adding that her source was Chris' sister. "Apparently, he was depressed. Co-workers were worried about him. He spent days watching the ice sheets break off and crash into the ocean. They found him in the bathtub…."

Melissa shut her eyes. It was horrible to envision someone mutilating themselves with a blade. Someone she had once loved and cared about very much.

She and Allison spent half an hour on the phone, catching up, making vague promises to get together. Then they ran out of things to say, and hung up. Melissa quietly cleaned up her lunch. Her husband would pick the kids

"Mayonaise" previously appeared in the *Adelaide Literary Magazine*.

up from school later that afternoon, giving her a few hours to herself. She decided to go dig through the crawl space in the attic.

She and Jack had finished the attic two years earlier, turning a dusty storage vault into a cozy, livable room. There was a home office set-up, a couch, and a TV. Melissa wedged herself into the crawl space, starting digging through the archives of her life, until she found the box with the yearbooks. The first yearbook she had ever acquired was a hard-bound, silver-covered junior high school *Torch*, 1995-96. Crisp, glossy pages. Black and white photos of everyone she had known in the world, age 13.

She brought the yearbook out of the crawl space and sat down on the couch. Flipped through the pages. Inscriptions decorated the inside covers, and many random pages, a multiverse of handwriting, scribbled in various colors of ink. She knew where Chris' inscription was, in the sports pages, toward the back, over the photo of the junior high alpine ski team. She found the photo and stared at it, remembering with crystal clarity the day it was taken. The whole team huddled together, sitting at the base of the practice hill at school, random skis sticking out of the snow. Fourteen kids on the team, seventh and eighth graders, all of them grinning like they had just laughed at the same joke. Her 13-year-old self, cherub-faced, with sharp brunette bangs, reclined on the snowy slope, her legs splayed out and half-buried, her upper body leaning against Chris. His hands rested on her head, like he was holding her hat in place.

His inscription read: "When I can, I will;" lyrics from "Mayonaise," the Smashing Pumpkins song, a concise note that belied the intensity of their feelings for each other. Many friends had written long, flowery testaments to the seventh grade, a year that ultimately had not mattered very much. But just five words from Chris.

She sometimes wondered if her memory was peculiar. She did not think of her life as a linear chain of experiences, the past a foggy haze at the end of the chain. For her, memory was more like a clear, amorphous orb. She remembered her entire life as if everything had occurred in the past couple of weeks. She remembered not only everyone she had known in junior high, but what they had looked like, sounded like, conversations she had had with them. So many details that her mind just refused to forget. Her marriage, the births of her children, her career, past relationships, friendships, school, college, vacations- everything existed in the same space, like a neat, orderly bookshelf, from which stories could be easily plucked.

She thought about that year on the ski team; riding creaky chairlifts up remote Maine mountains; the "whishing" sound of her skis on the slalom courses; eating chicken sandwiches and fries at McDonalds after a meet; the long bus rides home in the dark. Chris Ritter's easy smile, and calm, shoulder-clapping advice from the top of a mountain, as Melissa stared down a terrifying incline: "First rule: don't die."

She hunted through more boxes, unearthing her music collection. She pulled her old CDs from the box, inspected each one, stacked them on the table, until she found "Siamese Dream," by the Smashing Pumpkins. The plastic case still opened and closed, but the twin halves had broken and separated. The jacket with the song lyrics was so creased and bent it was nearly parchment. She pulled the jacket out and flipped through the lyrics.

"I'm going to put this on," she said to no one, indulging the habit she had developed of talking to herself when she was alone in the house. She put "Siamese Dream" in her stereo, pressed Play. A fresh injection of memories surged through her mind. She and Chris had listened to "Siamese Dream" dozens of times, passing the lyrics sheet back and forth, trying to decipher Billy Corgan's angsty poetry. Their favorite song on the album was the dark and mysterious "Mayonaise," a dirge of obscure promises. The song's opening bars took Melissa's heart to a place she could not explain, even twenty-five years after hearing it for the first time. The powerful explosion of guitar at 53 seconds plunged her straight into the bipolar years of '90s rock. Corgan took his time pulling you into the song—a masterpiece of sound recording—before his voice eventually arrived, like the whisper of God, bleeding secrets he would never suture. The refrain, "When I can, I will," seemed like a teary, desperate resolution to do something better. Melissa and Chris had spent hours debating the meaning of this song, the meaning of all the songs on "Siamese Dream." They laughed at their own fumbling interpretations. Corgan's lyrics were deeply personal, and profoundly opaque. The song titles—"Hummer," "Silverfuck," "Pissant"—were like inside jokes, laughing at the listener's insights. A song about love, or escape, or inadequacy, or who knows what, called "Mayonaise?"

"Maybe he was making a tuna fish sandwich," Chris suggested. "When the lyrics came to him."

Melissa lay on the floor, poking him with her socked toes, laughing up at the ceiling.

"Don't you want a pickle right now, for some reason?" he asked.

"Stop," she begged.

"That's all it is," Chris said. "He was hungry. Rock stars need protein too."

Later, after they had listened to "Mayonaise" maybe twenty times, Chris speculated that the lyrics "When I can, I will," perhaps meant that the singer, or the writer, or the voice, was telling someone that they were not perfect, and never would be, but all they could give, in their better moments, was their better self, and when they could, they would.

She listened to "Siamese Dream" all the way through, then started it over. She was glad her family would not be home for a while, would not find her quietly crying in the attic, over a long-estranged friend, before she had time to compose an explanation. Her mind flitted through countless winter memories of listening to music with Chris. But the memory she really wanted to relive was from the ski team.

It was January, 1996, a Saturday. The junior high alpine and Nordic ski teams had meets at Bleak Mountain, a jagged, rocky peak deep in Western Maine. Bleak Mountain only had two or three trails, one of which was just long enough for a slalom course. At the base of the slope sat a squat, wood-frame lodge. There was no chair lift, or even a T-bar, but only a rope-tow. Melissa had learned to ride rope-tows on the practice slope at school. You had to grab the moving rope, lean back, and squat, itself an effort of athleticism, and if you didn't lean back far enough, you'd be dragged. Everyone on the team duct-taped their gloves, to prevent the rope from shredding through the material and burning their hands.

The alpine competition comprised over a hundred skiers, each running two heats. The eighth graders went first, then the seventh graders. Melissa, Chris, Allison, and three or four other seventh graders spent the afternoon lurching up the hill in the falling snow, cruising the easy trail, waiting for their turn to race. By the time their competition began, the slalom had been run about two hundred times. A slim snake of ice wound downhill from the windy mountaintop to the lodge, the snow as firm and hard-packed as concrete. Melissa waited by the starting gate with her teammates, squinting through her goggles at the frozen course.

"This is crazy, man!" shouted Nick Barrett as he inched up to the starting gate. "It's sheer ice all the way to the bottom."

"Remember," said their coach, clouds of breath puffing around his head. "If you miss a gate, you're disqualified."

Nick Barrett clapped his poles together, screamed, and took off. Melissa watched Crazy Nick fly down the mountain, clipping gates, skis carving tight grooves in the snow. After what seemed like forever, he finally arrived at the bottom, cruising toward the lodge with his poles in the air.

Coach skied up to where Melissa and Chris stood shivering in the wind.

"Missy," Coach said. "About half of the girls ahead of you have already disqualified. All you have to do is complete the course, and you should place pretty well."

Chris clapped a hand on her shoulder. "No pressure."

"Just focus, and plant your poles, and you'll do fine," Coach said.

"I've never placed before," Melissa said to Chris.

"Me neither," Chris replied.

"I don't want to screw this up."

Chris' number was called. Before he stepped up to the gate, he turned to Melissa. "First rule," he said. "Don't die." The wind snapped around their ears like bullets, but Chris seemed perfectly calm.

"Don't die," Melissa repeated.

Chris waited for the signal, then took off. Allison stepped up beside Melissa. They huddled together against the wind, watching Chris weave down the course. He clipped the first few gates with expert precision, planting his poles and pivoting around the turns. Then he took a gate too wide, lost his balance, and wiped out, tumbling past the next two gates. Melissa held her breath as Chris careened out of control. But suddenly he hopped up and righted himself, skiing the rest of the course, even though he was disqualified. Melissa thought their second runs would be even worse.

She ran two heats down what was basically a luge course, and somehow miraculously finished them both. The key, she discovered, was to completely dismiss any particle of fear, to just fly. Crouch, tuck, plant, turn. Don't die.

At the end of her second heat, her heart pounding, she glided across the softer snow at the base of the mountain to the lodge. Fresh snow was falling, painting the mountain twilight-blue. She clacked off her skis and set them against the wall of the lodge.

Inside, the lodge was packed with the kids who had finished racing. Melissa found an empty seat at one of the long tables, peeled off her jacket, and sipped hot chocolate until the coaches arrived with the final results.

"Well, it was an ugly day," their coach said, laughing off what everybody already knew. "An icy course, but I'm proud of you all for running it. Some of you even finished."

Nick Barrett nudged Chris.

"We'll skip the disqualifications," Coach said. "And there were many. But we did manage to place three boys, and one girl, in the top ten." He read the names of the boys, all eighth graders, the usual suspects, who punched each other with snickering congratulations. "And our top lady racer was Missy Caouette, finishing eighth overall in the women's competition. You'll get your name in the paper, Miss."

The team swamped Melissa with cheers and hugs. Chris wrapped his arms around her shoulders and shouted: "Nobody touch her! We need her alive!"

It was a thrilling moment, but Melissa had never really liked public attention, and she felt more embarrassed than proud. It did feel good to have Chris' arms around her.

Darkness came quickly on Bleak Mountain, the snowstorm swallowing up the late-afternoon sun. Snow fell steadily as they loaded their gear back onto the bus for the return home. Melissa stared up at the black sky, the deceptively innocent snowflakes fluttering to the ground, the same icy substance that had tried to kill them on the slope.

The road home from Bleak Mountain led first, as always, to McDonalds, where the ski teams stuffed themselves with burgers and fries. Lumbering back onto the bus in her thick coat, boots, and snow pants, Melissa collapsed into her seat.

The last four rows of seats were packed tight with gear. The eighth graders crowded the seats as far back as they could get from the door, hiding from the coaches, conspiring. Melissa sat with the seventh graders toward the middle of the bus, their allotted territory. Placing eighth in the race drew her no closer to the cool kids, which was fine with her, since the cool kids intimidated her. Next year, if she was still on the team, she could sit at the back of the bus.

On the way to the meet, she had sat with Allison, the two of them whispering about the boys on the team, and the boys in their classes. Now Allison chose a seat near the front, where she could stretch out and go to sleep. Melissa watched Chris amble onto the bus with Crazy Nick and the other seventh-grade boys, staking out territory close to the girls, but separate. The boys started talking. The bus lurched into gear. Chris suddenly stood up and slipped into the seat beside her.

"I've never sat next to someone who placed before," he said.

She laughed. "I didn't die."

"That's the most important thing."

"*You* pretty much died though."

Chris shrugged, as if he hadn't really expected to win.

The bus hit a frost heave, and everyone cheered, their gear rattling onto the floor. Melissa jumped a few inches across the seat, nudging Chris. Chris started rooting through his backpack.

"Want to listen to some music?" he asked her.

"Sure," she said.

He fished a Walkman out of his backpack, untangled a length of wire with two ear buds. He handed her one of the buds.

"What is it?" she asked.

"A mix from the radio. I listen to 92-Moose when I'm doing home-work, and record the good songs when they come on. Some of the songs might be missing the first few seconds."

He tucked his ear bud into his ear, and Melissa did the same. The wires were short, forcing them to scooch up against each other. Chris turned up the volume, and they listened to the tinny music as conversation around the bus trickled to a hush.

One by one, everyone fell asleep. It took a while for the bus's heater to get cooking, but once it did, Melissa and Chris took off their jackets. Chris took out his ear bud and yawned. "I'm beat." He handed her his jacket. "Pillows."

Melissa bunched up their jackets and pressed them against the window. She removed her own ear bud, leaned against the jackets, felt the cool of the window through the puffy down. Chris put away his Walkman, slid over next to her. Without speaking, or explaining anything, he leaned his body across her lap, stretching his legs out into the aisle. Melissa's heart raced as he settled in against her. She glanced around the bus, to see if anyone was watching them, but no one was. Carefully she wrapped her arms around him, pulled him tight. He closed his eyes and let her hold him.

Melissa had never felt more excited, or more terrified. She had always wanted to hold a boy close to her. Suddenly she felt powerfully, almost murderously, protective of Chris. She almost wanted someone to interrupt them, to try to poke Chris, or steal his boots, or any of the other pranks they all endlessly pulled on each other, so that she could snap at them, lash out like a cobra, defend her boy.

The feeling did not pass. It strengthened into a concrete sense of purpose. She loved Chris, and would never let anything happen to him. She felt his warmth in all kinds of thrilling places, on her face, in her belly, in her breasts. In that moment, the world seemed perfectly aligned, with Chris in her arms, snow falling outside, and a long drive back to school. She understood, for the first time in her life, that love was as thick and blinding as a snowstorm, as relentless as an avalanche, entirely capable of swallowing her-crushing her—if she wasn't careful.

First rule, she told herself. *Don't die*

John Blahnik

ELDERPROOFING

Ron has always been a know-it-all, but retirement has made him worse. He no longer has sycophantic analysts to praise his brilliance, so now he shows off primarily to me.

At our dining room table, we take leisurely breakfasts. He reads *The Wall Street Journal* the way he has for years, holding the paper entirely open and perfectly upright. Each time he finishes a page, he crinkles the paper shut and then reopens it with a decisive snap. Sometimes he mutters a thoughtful "Hmm" or emits a displeased grunt. I thought that he developed this annoying habit out of nowhere, but then, sometime during our Brazil expat years, I realized that this was exactly how his boss read the paper.

"The con continues," Ron says in an amused voice, the voice of age condescending to youth.

He sets the paper on the table and smiles. Ron was never conventionally attractive, but he certainly once looked better than he does now. His face is round and fat. His hair and stubble are entirely white, but his eyebrows remain jet black. These days Ron, my husband of forty years, reminds me of a panda.

I spoon my soft-boiled egg. A financial lecture is imminent, but sometimes silence discourages it.

"Bitcoin has a reached a new high," says Ron. "I'm telling you, Margaret—it's the tulip mania of our time. Worse. At least when that bubble burst, the Dutch were left with flowers."

About to take a bite, I hold my spoon steady. I struggle to summon the right memory, an increasingly common occurrence.

"You've always been against Bitcoin, right?" I ask.

"And all other cryptocurrencies."

"But since you last criticized it, Bitcoin has appreciated."

Ron frowns. "True."

"So had you invested, you would have made money. Bitcoin, for the period of time you've been against it, has been a good investment. Today's financial news proves that. Right?"

Ron's lips part with a moist smack, but he doesn't speak. Smiling, I eat my egg.

Ron needs a good hobby. Since we left Brazil to retire in Greenwich, he has picked up and dropped cycling, golf and sailing. I was optimistic when he took up oenology. Brazil taught us how to do two things—to speak passable Portuguese and to drink at all hours of the day. I hoped that Ron and I could lose ourselves in connoisseurship. But suddenly I couldn't handle wine. It all had an acrid taste, and instead of getting tipsy, I simply got hungover. Ron sold our wine cases at a loss.

His latest hobby, if I can even call it that, is my least favorite: Ron's obsessed with our health. He believes that septuagenarians must respect their circadian rhythms. He has established a schedule to encourage good "sleep hygiene." At eight thirty, our phones buzz, reminding us to restrict liquids so that our shrinking bladders don't awaken us. At ten we are in bed, and our white noise machine is droning. At seven the next morning, our automated bedroom lights turn on, at first dim and then bright, mimicking sunrise.

Ron's obsession would be tolerable if it were primarily limited to his unconscious hours. But throughout the day he is overly aware of exercise and diet. He buys bought me a pedometer, and if before dinner I haven't gotten sufficient steps, he takes me for a walk. That's what he calls it, as if I were his dog. Ron discourages me from snacking, and more and more often, he does our cooking. His meals are low in salt, low in butter and low in pleasure.

I dread his mackerel. When it appears on my plate—steam rising from its gray, papery skin; an intense odor filling the dining room—I grimace. Ron sits across from me, and I keep looking at the mackerel's head. Its mouth hangs open, as if even the fish were shocked by its smell.

Ron clears his throat. "Have a bite. It's an acquired taste. You just need to eat it a few more times."

I frown. He speaks He has spoken to me in the same tone we once used with Charlie, our only child, back when he was a picky eater.

"It's full of Omega Threes," continues Ron. "Excellent for memory."

"Is that a benefit?" I ask. "What if I want to forget its taste?"

Many years ago, Ron found my sarcasm funny. Later, he found it abrasive. These days I don't know what he thinks. He responds to it either with silence or with more pedantry.

Leaning over the table, he lectures me on the benefits of polyunsaturated fats, particularly those found in fish. He gestures with his fork, the same way a college professor might gesture with a piece of chalk.

"*The New England Journal of Medicine* published a study that tracked a group of Sicilians who ate mackerel everyday of their lives. You know what became of them?"

He pauses for emphasis.

"They all died of dietary boredom?" I ask.

"They became centenarians, every single one of them."

Ron sits back looking pleased, as if convinced that my enthusiasm for mackerel will now adjust to the correct level. He thinks that the goal of retirees should be to live as long as possible, to live so that they can keep doing—what, exactly?

I too could use a hobby. When Ron was working in Brazil, I was always busy. I spent weekdays managing our household staff and volunteering at Charlie's international school. On weekends, I took Charlie to the country club, where we socialized with other expat families. But as I got older, my world evaporated. The men retired, and my friends left Brazil to return to cities scattered across the US and the delete the Europe. Charlie took a job on Wall Street, and though we moved to Greenwich to be closer to him, he soon left New York to seek his fortune in Asia.

For what felt like too long, Charlie hardly called. But recently he calls me most days, either before work or right after. He wears a button down and a tie, and behind him is the nighttime cityscape of his new home.

Hong Kong?

He tells me about trading options, puts and calls, about trading not stocks, exactly, but the future ability to trade stocks, and I become a mute. Charlie sounds like Ron, as if he were less interested in holding a conversation than in performing a monologue. I try not to think about how the child I understood so well is becoming a man whom I increasingly don't.

"Tell me about your social life," I interject.

Charlie loosens his tie, smirks. His dimples remind me of the boy whom I could make laugh on command by saying "Thirty-three, thirty-three! Dirty tree, dirty tree!" I feel a quiet optimism, a feeling similar to the one I get on the rare occasion that I learn a far-off friend will visit me.

Charlie laughs. "Why don't you ask the question we both know you want to ask?"

"Are you dating anyone?"

Charlie's silence feels coy.

"No," I say, "I can't believe it. Who is she?"

"Another expat whose firm also transferred her to Singapore." Charlie swivels in his chair. "Erica! Come meet my mom."

A dark-skinned girl, who could very well be Brazilian, enters the room. She gives me the warm smile that so many Brazilians seem born with and that we expats could never master.

"For how long has Charlie been hiding you from me?"

Charlie turns to her. "Well, we officially started dating yesterday, but the first time we—"

They both laugh. I know I should be scandalized, but I'm pulsing with joy. My smile tires my cheeks.

"Things move fast in Hong Kong," I say.

Charlie purses his lips. "Singapore, Mom. You know that."

Ron's obsession with health has developed into a desire to prepare for our future as invalids. He says that our clapboard colonial is too large, that even with help from weekly cleaners and landscapers, the upkeep will tax our eventual frail bodies. He says that the narrow doorways, the stairs and the bathtubs will make the house unlivable if one of us ends up in a wheelchair. Companies specialize in outfitting homes for geriatric life, and Ron hires one named *Sunset Solutions*.

We spend the weeks it outfits our home at a spa in the Berkshires. The spa is a mansion that once belonged to a robber baron, but I dislike it. The staff wears all white, and I can't help but think of nurses and orderlies. Each morning Ron takes me to an exercise studio where a Russian woman has me strengthen my thighs with a barrel hoop. Each afternoon he takes me for my walk on the estate's winding, verdant trails. Each evening, to improve my sleep, he insists that I do group meditation.

This is an activity that I especially dislike. The point of meditation, according to my spandex-wearing male guru, is to exit today's overstimulated world. But my world has too little stimulation. It could use more. The class sits crossed-legged on folded blankets, and the guru tells everyone to clear their minds. I don't listen. A stick of incense burns, its rising smoke twisted like a signature. The room smells of sandalwood. I let my mind wander to thoughts of Charlie. He lives abroad. Brazil? No. But he has a girlfriend—a beautiful, charming girlfriend. The guru tells us to bring our attention to our breath. I feel my chest slowly rise and fall. For the rare moment at this spa, I am relaxed.

Back in Brazil, when I was pregnant with Charlie, Ron and I child-proofed our home. We had our staff install baby gates at the top and bottom of stairs, snap safety covers over electric outlets and move tall, wobbly floor lamps into storage. Today *Sunset Solutions* has completed a process that its contractor unironically calls elderproofing. She is a short, stocky woman, and explaining her work in our living room, she again and again uses that ugly word. Ron is immune to it. He keeps nodding as if he were an eager student in a lecture hall.

She takes us on a tour of her work. In the living room, she has repositioned light switches so that they can be turned on and off from the sectional. In the kitchen, she has placed no-slip rubber backings on our rug. In one downstairs bathroom, she installed an elevated toilet. She has me sit on it, and my feet don't touch the floor. I think of Charlie in his booster chair. The most significant change to our house is by our stairs. We now have an elevator. The three of us board it, and as it rumbles up, Ron grins at me as if he has gifted me some exciting luxury. I roll my eyes.

The elevator chimes. The doors open, and Ron and I follow the contractor to our en-suite bathroom. Where our clawfoot bathtub once stood, there is now a glass walk-in shower. It has French doors, and opening them, the contractor walks in. She extends her arms by her sides, pirouettes in the doorway and addresses me with pride.

"You have enough space here for two wheelchairs."

"Lovely," I say. "Ron and I will be able to take our romantic joint showers even when we're cripples."

Ron scoffs. "I know you find this ridiculous, Margaret—but I'm just following the facts. According to the Mayo Clinic, fifty-nine percent of elders spend at least one month in a wheelchair. Not hedging for that possibility is foolish."

It occurs to me that Ron thinks that old age is a problem like any other, one that he can solve with statistics and money.

"Let's show her something she'll like," he says to the contractor, and we all enter the bedroom.

The contractor takes Ron's phone, opens a program and presses a button. Something in the upstairs hallway makes an electronic beep and then a sustained hum that sounds like a distant cicada. Ron and the contractor watch the bedroom's open doorway. The hum gets louder. A short, black, circular machine rolls itself into the bedroom. Its front has tiny bristles that look like centipede legs. It keeps going straight, collides with the dresser and stops. It spins in place and then rolls toward the bed.

"It's a robotic vacuum," says Ron. "We bought a fleet of them. We'll no longer have to waste time tidying up between Luisa's visits."

The vacuum collides with the bed and stops. It spins in place, rolls itself toward the dresser, collides with the dresser, again stops. I glance at the contractor. I raise my eyebrows.

"I promise you'll be impressed in the future," she says. "Right now it's learning the room's dimensions."

The vacuum continues colliding with the bed and dresser.

"It's a slow learner," I say.

I can't return to sleep. The bedroom is filled with darkness, and the white noise machine silences all other sounds. Lying beside my sleeping husband, I have nothing to do but get lost in my thoughts.

I want to remember yesterday's conversation with Charlie, but at night, my memories behave perversely. The distant ones feel recent, and the recent ones feel distant. His girlfriend was there again, that I am sure of, and I saw them exchange that look that they often do, that look that says they are amazed that one person could be this perfect. I was so happy. And then they told me about their lives in—here my memory fails me. I know the answer, but searching for it is like searching a lake for a lost ring. I see a wavering glint, but reaching for it, I stir up silt, and the water goes opaque. I keep searching and keep failing. The white noise sounds like the static of my muddled mind.

I have an urge to leave the bedroom.

Ron dislikes when I act on this urge. He sometimes catches me outdoors, strolling our garden at night, and each time he lectures me on the importance of uninterrupted sleep and insists that I return to bed.

I scoot away from him, toward the bed's edge, watching his dark outline for signs of alertness. Careful not to jounce the bed, I step onto the carpet. I can see just enough to walk. That set of shadows is our chairs and coffee table. The long, single shadow is our dresser. That horizontal bar of dim light marks the bottom of the door. But opening the door, I see, in the hallway's gray light, an elevator. A pang of anxiety strikes me.

I have no idea where I am.

Wherever I am, it is somewhere I never intended to be. I feel that I am trapped in some place of commerce—Ron's office building, a shopping mall—and that I am alone, locked in after hours. My heartbeat quickens. My nightgown sticks to a patch of sweat. I can no longer focus on a single thought, and this haze makes me even more anxious.

"Margaret?"

This is Ron. He is a dim silhouette standing in front of a pitch-black room. From out that room comes constant, unpleasant static. I back away from it.

"We talked about this," he says. "You can't stroll the garden when you should be sleeping."

I don't want to go into that room. But more than anything, I don't want to remain lost and alone. I let Ron take my hand.

Sometimes I forget how to answer Charlie's calls. My computer repeats the same pattern of dings, and I sit there, confused, until Ron answers it for me.

Charlie tells us a story about an acquisition he engineered. It is late, and the room is dark. My eyes feel heavy. Illuminated by the computer's blue glow, Ron remains attentive. He seems proud of Charlie, and so am I, though for what I can't exactly say. Charlie works for—I can't remember. And lives in—Brazil? Yes. Charlie is a banker, and he owns a grand, fully-staffed house.

I smile. The back-and-forth between my boys is indecipherable, filled with jargon, but I like listening to their voices. It gives me a safe, comfortable feeling—the feeling I would get when, as a child, during dinner parties, I sat beneath the dining room table.

A dark-skinned girl appears behind Charlie. She notices me, waves and walks off camera. I interrupt Charlie and Ron.

"Who was that?" But then I know the answer. "Is she your domestic?"

Charlie tilts his head, opens his mouth, but doesn't speak. He then laughs. "That was Erica, my girlfriend. Erica, come say hi to my parents."

The dark-skinned girl returns and waves again. I realize that I have met her many, many times. I blush. I feel tongue-tied. She and Charlie trade words that are too quiet to hear, and then she is giving me a warm, forgiving smile.

"It's my haircut," she says. "Plenty of people can't recognize me now that it's short."

"Erica's almost running Gaia Capital," says Charlie. "If one of us has enough money to boss the other one around, it's Erica."

"Tell us a Gaia story," says Ron.

They all move past my mistake, discuss Erica's demanding job, but I remain too mortified to speak. Charlie and Erica say goodbye, and I force a smile. I drop it when they are no longer on the computer. From the corner of an eye, I see Ron look at me with oppressive concern.

"She didn't care, Margaret. The important thing is that you remember her now."

I keep looking at the computer. It shows a picture of young Charlie on the beaches of Natal. Ron wanted to take Charlie to go parasailing, to ride dune buggies, to visit colonial sites, but Charlie only wanted to play with a stray beach dog. Digger. That's what Charlie named him.

"You do remember Erica, right?" says Ron, and when I continue ignoring him, he elaborates. "For over a year, she's been dating Charlie, our son."

I glare at Ron. "I know who Charlie is."

"I'm just trying to help."

He places a hand on my shoulder, and I shrug it off.

"You can help by not treating me like a child."

I have almost made it outside.

At night, the downstairs seems strange. Tall windows cast the living room in a pale, blue light. The kitchen's white marble seems to glow. Walking on tiles, my bare feet feel unusually cool. I hear a quiet hum and stop to listen. It gets louder. It sounds like a summer night, like the electric buzz of invisible insects.

A line of four short, circular somethings parades into the living room. Their centers have small red lights, as if they were Olympic torch-bearers, and breaking file, they perform what could be a slow, choreographed dance, dancing first around the living room and then around the kitchen. One of them brushes against my foot. Its front has whisker-like bristles, and I feel happy, as if a friendly pet is sniffing me. The dancers re-form their line and parade out. The hum fades.

I am in my kitchen.

But why?

I open the refrigerator, and the white light stings my eyes. I scan drinks, yogurts, plastic leftover containers and cellophane-wrapped fish. Nothing comes to me.

"Margaret?"

As I see Ron behind me, my stomach tightens. I have a feeling similar to being in a good dream turning bad—a nameless anxiety. Explaining to Ron why I am in the kitchen seems essential.

"I was just—" I say, but no other words come.

Ron keeps waiting, and my mind remains empty.

"Going for a nighttime walk?" he offers.

His tone is of a helpful teacher saving a struggling student. Yes, I remember, the garden. Ron keeps smiling at me, and the nameless anxiety begins to dissipate.

"Do you mind you mind if I come along?" he asks.

"No," I say, "please do."

He extends his hand, and I take it.

We open the backyard door. The air has the crisp, earthy smell of fall. A thin layer of fog hovers above the garden. Ron and I step into the moonlit night.

Author's Note

"Elderproofing" began as a sketch narrated in the third person about a husband who copes with his wife's dementia by becoming pedantic. But when I finished writing it, I realized that I was primarily interested in the wife. She was funnier and more affecting. I wanted to tell a new story from her point of view. I worried (and still worry?) that readers might find this perspective too disorienting, but taking that perspective felt crucial to capturing her character and experience.

Christopher Locke

CREATION MYTH

Nothing made Lorraine feel more alive than rainstorms. The roof applauded like a concert hall as water streamed the windows and gut-busted the drains. The bird bath tilted its head like a patient drooling. Fog settled between the elms and filled the backyard like a summer cookout. Lorraine missed the summer; she thought about last July and the blue dress her boyfriend gave her, satin ribbon announcing its surprise. That night, she told her husband Jasper she bought it on a whim—*Lord & Taylor* had a sale. She'd barely had enough time to change the sheets before he came home, but Jasper was pleased with how the dress hung from her shoulders and accentuated her neck as she turned in the light of his approval.

Lorraine now opened the front door and stepped barefoot into all that weather; the deluge made it seem like she had entered a giant, primordial room: the air coursed with hundreds of wet thumbprints touching every inch of her body, and shrubs and flowers and vines spattered loosely around her like wallpaper sloughing off. Rivulets drained under her feet as she walked onto the prickly tar and down the driveway.

Her hair clung to her forehead like plastic wrap. Lorraine pushed her bangs aside as she stepped into the middle of the road and walked the yellow line, away from the house and all its small sufferings. Her black bra became visible under her white t-shirt. Lorraine closed her eyes and put her hands out at either side, imagining a tight rope. She teetered, but Lorraine knew no one could save her.

She counted to ten and stopped. When Lorraine opened her eyes, she felt born and then reborn, several lives in a single moment as thick streams ran muddy on either side of the road—a sluice of anxious sticks and desiccated leaves tipping up and under a flow going somewhere Lorraine could only dream of.

Earlier, her boyfriend sat in his truck and cried when she told him it was over. Right there in the parking lot of the Circle K. Lorraine was repulsed by his weakness. *What did I do wrong? How can I make this right?* was all he would say, and he tried to hold her hand and she kept pulling it away. *Nothing*, she said. *You disgust me.* Which made him cry harder until she had to get out and call an Uber to get home. Waiting for her ride, Lorraine sat at a table inside next to the hotdog rollers and heard the old timers talk about the upcoming storm. *Should be a doozy*, said a man tufted under a green baseball cap. His coffee steamed his chin as he smiled and laughed. Sipped.

Lorraine stepped off the road and swung her leg over a guardrail still warped by the Halloran boy after he shattered his parents' SUV last Easter. Glass littered the road like diamonds and each morning Loraine went out to sneak a call to her boyfriend she wondered how much they would be worth if real. After a week they vanished, and Lorraine was afraid someone knew she'd been eyeing them.

Stepping down the loose embankment, she heard thunder and was disappointed the rain was lighter in the woods; all those trees throwing their arms up to catch whatever the sky offered. She came down to a boy-sized culvert and peered inside. It was dank until the end shined a perfect circle in the middle of all that blackness, like at the beginning of those James Bond movies Jasper loved so much.

After he found out about the boyfriend, Jasper took the boys and left for his mother's downstate in Utica. Lorraine wanted to stop him but she felt she had already lived through that moment before, and that she would continue to live it, would continue to hear Jasper curse and smash an armload of groceries onto the ground, tub of banana yogurt cracking open like an infant's skull; the note he waved at her like a gun that the boyfriend sent him, telling him about his love for Lorraine and that he refused to be silent anymore; the way the boys cowered against the living room door in the heat of Jasper's rage, Lorraine holding up her hands like he was a levee; the tires spitting rocks as the *Denali* tore away from the house and the boys crying through the car windows at her; and later, the methodical way she took down the Thanksgiving decorations she'd hung with her sons, placing them neatly in the woodstove for later.

Lorraine ducked low and crept into the culvert. She hunched and moved slowly until she got to the middle. Rainwater streamed around her ankles. She remembered how she'd bathe the boys when they were infants, making sure the water was just warm enough but not scalding. How they looked up at her with nothing but belief. Their trust was unbearable.

Her shins and the bottom of her ass were now in water. The growing current mumbled, and sticks began touching her. Every raindrop that pushed past her took something else away. *Is this what it means to be forgiven*, she thought. In Bible school as a kid, her favorite story was about the

Great Flood—all that mockery and denial until it was too late, helpless fists pounding the ark doors. Lorraine closed her eyes and braced herself against the corrugated sides. She wondered how long she could stay there, quiet inside the Earth. For a day. A week. Or until the night animals found her, picked at what was left.

L.S. Engler

SCENT OF SUMMER

Diane had always been skeptical about love, such an elusive entity, one she wasn't sure even existed. She'd heard about it plenty; some people never shut up about it. But, whenever she tried to capture it for herself, it always escaped her. Everyone said she was trying too hard. You couldn't force it or will it into being; it was just supposed to *happen*, usually when you weren't expecting it, usually when you stopped looking for it, but that hadn't worked either. Nothing in life ever *just happened*. Nothing worthwhile. You always had to work for the good stuff.

But then, just like they said, it did happen, when she had just about given up—when her fingers pinched that last straw. As sure as the melting snow, the lengthening of days, the return of the robins to their messy little nests, spring swept in with the promise of something new. It arrived in the breath of a tropical breeze, sun-kissed highlights, and orange citrus scent. Diane sat in the park outside her office on the first warm day suggesting summer, eating her lunch and hoping to clear her head of the abysmal daily grind. The wind rustled through the leaves of the trees, and she looked up from her tuna on toast, her vegetable soup, and there was Cora.

Cora was a typhoon, a churning burst of energy and light that floated by untethered. No. Not floating; she was falling, attempting to catch an errant Frisbee. "I got it, I got it!" she called out, shifting, shifting, and then finally making the grab for the battered yellow disc, unaware of the unsuspecting Diane right in the way.

In the blink of an eye, she had spilled half of her soup on the woman suddenly in her lap where her sandwich used to be. Fleetingly, Diane was furious, but as soon as Cora started to laugh, Diane laughed, too, shaken by the absurdity of the situation.

"I'm so sorry." Cora scrambled to her feet, brushing crumbs off her butt, holding out her soup-dampened shirt. "Looks like lunch is on me. Let me make it up to you."

Diane thought she was joking, accepting the apology with a chorus of, "No, it's fine, it's okay." But Cora was adamant, not allowing Diane to leave until arrangements for amends had been made. Diane allowed it only because she didn't have time to argue—a quick glance at her watch told her she needed to get headed back to work. But a curious churning grew in her stomach as she rode the elevator up to her floor, not gnawing hunger from her interrupted lunch, but something else. The feeling grew worse as their Saturday lunch loomed closer. Was it anticipation, or had she simply caught a springtime bug? Could it be excitement, or was it just indigestion?

During that first lunch, Cora was able to unravel all of Diane's tightly held reservations with the ease of her smile. She couldn't remember the last time she could talk so openly with another person or when someone's company was just so pleasant. Cora oozed summertime sweetness, melting away Diane's naturally cold disposition. She worried that their personalities would eventually start to clash, but they complimented each other, and Diane was enthralled by their differences, among many other things.

The blossoming of spring mirrored their relationship, smoothing out into something comfortable and lazy in the heat of summer. But summer eventually faded, too, and the new feeling in Diane's stomach was unpleasant and empty. No more warm light slipping through her windows, no more spilled watercolor landscapes of the setting sun. The song of laughter and lawn mowers and ice cream trucks was coming to its end—no more charcoal in the air or sweat on the glass of lemonade. Even with everything that made summer so sweet and succulent, shucking corn and that first juicy bite of watermelon, what she missed most was how the sun kissed Cora's cheeks, making her freckles pop out like stars across the sky; how everything made her sleepy, and how they'd cuddle together despite the damp, humid stickiness of their bodies.

Fall was not without its merits, though, casting everything in bronze and gold, the same shades of Cora's wild curly hair. Diane tried to hold on as the weather began to cool, as crisp autumn marched relentlessly toward an unforgiving winter, but no matter how tightly she gripped, the ice crept up and spread, blanketing the world in soft angel dust. Cora turned as cold as the bitter air; restless with the endless lack of color. Nothing seemed to make her laugh anymore; she drifted away when Diane reached out. *White on the ground, white in the sky, white, white, white.* Cora said it made her feel crazy, so she escaped to warmer climates, tropical, distant, alone.

Just like that, as swiftly as she'd come in, Cora was gone, taking summer with her, as well as the person Diane thought she'd met that bright and sunny day. Diane had that first bite of love, but all that remained was an awful, bitter aftertaste. Even when the weather started to warm again, she'd catch the faint scent of oranges or the flash of a yellow Frisbee, and her nose would wrinkle with distaste. Fair-weather, fickle love that fled at the first brush of cold. She no longer questioned the existence of love, but sometimes felt that she preferred her previous ignorance.

Until a whiff of coconut lotion and a lightly strummed guitar turned her head. She dropped a few coins into the busker's hat when she got up to return to work—back to the grind, and he smiled at her. It made her shiver, despite the sweat clinging to her back, and the door that love had barely just closed swung open again, letting in that same summer breeze that invaded all her sense and reason. She hesitated, and then she smiled, asking for the name of his song.

Q&A WITH ROBERT ZALLER

Our featured poet, Robert Zaller, took some time to respond to questions from Publisher and Editor-in-Chief of *Schuylkill Valley Journal*, Peter Krok.

Peter Krok: In the poems "Marsyas" and "The Death of Polycrates," I see the subject as hubris. In both poems you draw on figures of the ancient world. In all this there is also the indifference of humankind. In fact, you are very drawn to the ancient world and mythology. I presume you see lessons in these Greek figures for us today.

Robert Zaller: Greek history and mythology have always been important to my outlook on the world, and Greece itself—the landscape, the people—a part of my life. My late wife, Lili, and the children we raised, have been the essence of it. Marsyas is of course a figure in mythology, who challenged the God Apollo and was flayed alive in punishment for it. The poem itself was inspired by Titian's painting of the scene. Polycrates was a Greek tyrant of the late sixth century BCE, and his death as recorded is evoked in the poem. Hubris, yes, but power is an underlying subject in both poems.

PK: You are a noted scholar, writer and poet. One need only check Wikipedia or google your name to see the breadth of your work. A question: how did you come to write poetry? Few scholars have your commitment to poetry. Was it the influence of Lili Bita, who I should add is a celebrated Greek poet and actress and was your wife of many years? I believe Lili has profoundly influenced and inspired you. You have translated her work. How do you see her as an influence in your writing?

RZ: I think it's fair to say that we birthed each other as poets. Lili had published a book of stories in her late teens that was praised by the celebrated Greek writer Nikos Kazantzakis, but began to write poetry only after we met. She wrote of course in her native Greek, and asked me to translate it. Doing this with her inspired me to try my own hand at verse. I found I had it in me, and kept on going.

I continued to translate Lili's poetry to the end of her life, and her stories and memoirs as well. Her style and thought were unique to her, and it was deeply enriching to me to enter her world, a part of our intimacy. It was her world, though, and as a poet I have had mine.

PK: As an aside, I want to mention, your two love poems for Lili in this selection are so moving. In "Stealing Figs," you write,

> Your eyes are the first stars
> of the night
> and I am proud as any Adam.

And in "Anniversary" there are your lines,

> The story's finished.
> Time can run backward
> if it chooses …
> Still, somewhere,
> two lovers meet again
> for their hour.

There is no more to say than to read these testaments of your love.

There too is your deep appreciation of Robinson Jeffers. Besides being the author and editor of collections of essays on Jeffers, you have written two studies of him: *The Cliffs of Solitude* and *Robinson Jeffers and the American Sublime.* Your titles express a great deal. Why did you choose the titles? Jeffers was a stoic and wrote about the natural landscape and you do the same. What is the influence of Jeffers in your work?

RZ: I discovered Jeffers by accident—incidentally, while in Greece, which he too wrote about greatly. At the time, he was a poet few people remembered, but the first half dozen lines of his I read hooked me for good, and I have been pondering and writing about him ever since. So have others. "The Cliffs of Solitude" came to me as a title that expressed his personal as well as poetic character. The other title is straightforward, since the subject of that book interprets him through the Romantic notion of the sublime in its American variant. Doubtless Jeffers has influenced my own work, but that's for others to say. I can only say that I am grateful for whatever I have learned from him.

PK: In the landscape of many of your poems, one finds stones, pebbles, rocks. I could say they are imbedded in your work. There is a timeless quality aspect in these things. They endure. They were before us and will be after us. They, in their own way, are all part of the natural world. Why do they have so much interest to you?

You also write so much about the sea and above all its islands. And in the background to this I think there is "Silence." Islands play a significant part. Are the frequent references to islands actually indicative of how you see yourself?

RZ: I'd have to say that no man is an island, but some people are island-lovers and I am certainly one. Each is a unique and distinct part of the earth, and each, in its distinctive form, flora, and fauna, has offered me a different world. Stones have for me a similar quality, and in their hardness an integrity of their own.

PK: I remember when you read your "Dresden Zoo." I felt the earth almost shake with the poundings and stress of the emotion in that poem. The poem explodes with your dramatic voice. What inspired you to write that poem?

RZ: "The Dresden Zoo" was a response to the firebombing of Dresden at the end of World War II, and what I found about the fate of the zoo animals trapped by the blaze. It was probably the most controversial bombing of the war after Hiroshima and Nagasaki, at least on the Allied side. But it is really a poem about the tragedy of warmaking itself, and the responsibility we all bear for it.

PK: Your style is to be spare and let us say you rather avoid the metaphor and express a quiet intensity because you are interested in a more direct expression in your poetry. Could you elaborate a bit on how you see your style?

RZ: I've never given a thought to my style. I try to say what I have to say in the way I need to say it. Obviously, I had models when I started out, but I had to arrive at myself. Slowly, I might add.

PK: I believe you are interested in Samuel Beckett. Could you share if there are other writers that influenced you and perhaps give a short comment on why.

RZ: Beckett influenced everybody. He influenced my plays when I started writing them, but one day I wrote a farce and that was that. After that I was on my own. Plays are speech. A dramatic voice is different from any other kind, and you have to find your own for that too.

I admired Pablo Neruda's voice very much, but I always carried Willis Barnstone's book of modern European poets when I traveled. One day at a seafront restaurant in Athens a stranger came up to us. He turned out to be Barnstone, and he asked my wife Lili if she were Lili Bita. She said yes, and he replied that he'd recognized her from the jacket photo of her own first book of poems. So I can't say whether Lili influenced Barnstone, a poet himself. But she obviously impressed him.

PK: I admit that I am often puzzled by your poems:

> Born under the plunge of the sun, their frailty,
> like ours, dies with the light.
> Their single flaw makes distance real.
> They are the riddle that solves the night.

Could you explain a bit the meaning, as you see it, in the lines?

RZ: The subject is islands, which have always had fascination for me. had to express myself here in terms of paradox. You can't unpack a paradox without ruining it, at least in poetry, at least for me. All I can say is that the poem is a fusion of observation and imagination, and that I hope the whole poem makes the context clearer.

THE DEATH OF POLYCRATES

The sun mounts over bare hills
Asian before it is Greek
From here one can see
where the tyrant was crucified
on the Persian shore opposite.
He writhed like a snake
nailed to a post.
Some of his Greeks no doubt watched
and some, lighting fires, rejoiced.
Polycrates could see from where he hung
the city he had ruled
the strong walls of the harbor
the great aqueduct
the goddess' temple
that were all wonders of the world
in that simple time
so impressed with feats of stone.
It was all there before him,
all he had built,
reared again
in the shimmer of his agony.

Who kills a king
is damned into immortality
who kills a tyrant
shares his shabby end.
Alexander came and cleansed the coast
and Romans, Goths, Venetians, Turks
the tyrant's ruins peep out now
between the summer villas
and his name, once inscribed in marble,
sells postcards and plastic souvenirs.
But still the question nags:
did this man die well?
Did the animal reclaim him
or did power hold sway

outstaring its fate
and the twisted flesh become its own monument
stone with the stone it had raised to glory?
But no one remembers a tyrant well
and no stone tells all it knows.

MARSYAS

                    Marsyas,
under the careful paring,
is still alive. King Midas looks down
with an interest partly clinical,
partly compassionate: his sandaled foot,
shapely despite age, wiggles
in fellow feeling; his pensive head
rests on a hand tapered with rings.
The golden-haired girl slices meticulously.
Marsyas hangs head downward in the dust,
his eyes screaming more than his mouth
for he breathes too and his bruised throat
can make no sound but a ragged panting
that drags itself over a vocable
like a body over a spike.

                    Apollo
is not present at all;
he has turned away, satisfied
in justice but repelled by cruelty,
which is what leers
from the mortal and bestial eyes.
Midas is neither god nor man:
intellectual, he speculates on pain,
he weighs and analyzes, he learns from it.
His notes will be of use to us,
for he detects the hidden note of beauty
in Marsyas' scraped howl,
he understands that a whole body
can become a lute under the right scalpel.

                    Finally
when only dust motes
dance from the vacancy of a mouth
whose lips, too, have been picked clean
by the knife, when Marsyas is only an echo
that screams that screams that screams

Midas folds up his notepad, rises
on suave haunches and expels a sigh
which at a distance could be mistaken for pity
but is, he would certainly assure you,
no more than the sound
of a book closing on its subject.

THE SILENCE OF THE ISLAND

I walk
the silence of the island.
The west
fills with light.
Each stone
takes its benediction.
A tethered goat
bleats on the hill.
A bird
startles a tree
with three fierce notes.
The wind drones,
and the sea,
working its passage,
rests an oar
on the rush of time.
All this
is the silence
of the island,
the core of its dreaming,
the secret stillness.
Here speech sinks into itself,
the finally unsaid.

LET LIGHT ATTEND

Let light attend, the poet said
where heat parts dawn
to let strict sky in
for the climb
that unfurls the world's display
opening for us
the perfection of the day.
They lie there then
jeweling the blue
the proud boats at anchor
having circumnavigated by night
the globe's wide sea.
Never by an inch
do they miss their berths.
Nothing's out of place,
chuckles the wind.
Nothing rides me,
says the wave.
The sun's rays
are nailed to their posts
and where your step ends
it has just begun.
The light deceives as always,
and where have you, O dreamer, been?

THE ISLANDS APPEAR

In the evening the islands appear
faint blue incisions on the parchment of night
coming each day to live their hour
between the red sun's fall and the evening star.
Sea and sky are perfect,
the dying sun marries them.
Pure volume, lucid height.
Yet without islands there is no solace.
Born under the plunge of the sun, their frailty,
like ours, dies with the light.
Their single flaw makes distance real.
They are the riddle that solves the night.

ENOUGH OF THE SKY

The angel spoke:
haven't you had
enough of the sky?
Not yet,
was my reply.
Haven't you had
enough of the sea?
No, I said,
it still flows
from Homer to me.
The angel smiled
and stepped aside.
That was the last
I knew.

THE DRESDEN ZOO

The horses heard it first
the first shudder of earth
tensed the tasseled ankles
the first rush of air
shook the gilded manes
and suddenly they felt
the milky odor of fear
that emanated from walls
the restless clangor of flagpoles
the weakening of the moon.
In the cobbles of the Altstadt
a thousand year fear was forming
the fear called Holocaust
the fear called Judgment
fear leaped in blue sparks
from telephones
fear gripped the knives
in their cupboards
a whole city was lightly trembling
and the sweat that drenched the angel
of Dresden Cathedral
broke from the flanks of the horses.
Only the sirens were silent
only those-to-die of Dresden
heard nothing
until the trumpet of fear
sounded from the blind throat
and gave the city its voice.

A parliament of fires
caped the city
in one gathered breath
mounting the stair
curling into kitchens
snuffing the small frenzy
of breath in the cellar.

Women mad with gaiety
shed dung in the fountains
clowns and donkeys
vied for the trapeze
and wild mares, terror-sleeked,
drank the black heat
that burst their lungs.
The city disrobed
to put on new garments.
All of silk and silver
must shed, all of copper, of brass

all of duralex, isinglass, manganese, stone
all bars, angles, scabbards, grids
all terminated geometries
all multiple anfracts
all banners, esplanades, prospects
whisperings, melodies, facts
all shrubbery, placards, wine
tacks, dolls, pills, tops, teeth
all texts, contracts, bills of lading
all starvation, optimism, truth
all bolsters, ligatures, corsets, struts
all cambric, tinfoil, bunting
all pylons, fulcra
joists, beams
vectors, polygons, crossties
all tremors, all shadows, all lusts.
Purged street by street
stone by stone
Dresden stepped forth
from skin, from flesh, from bone
and naked in the terror
of her wild false dawn
put on a cerement of flame.

In the Grosser Garten
the velvet panther
prowls his acre of instinct

tirelessly circling
the unslaked fury
of his stringent eye.
The llama, as in a dream,
beholds his uncome death
in an eternal mirage of terror
stalker and prey
mirrored in a destiny
without consummation.
Shall the day come
that pardons claw and flesh
shall the blood flow
that slakes this desperate innocence?
The doors, the seals stand open
freedom beckons
in a blaze of light
and tyrannous angels guard
the pathways of the jungle
with aisles of flame.
Stumbling into the world's last hour
the beasts seek the door of paradise
that is before history.
In deep grass
the bait of fire is laid
tall trees vouch the descending sky
sweeping their trunks with palms of agony
till the molten pressure of heaven
flings them down in writhing torches
that curse the ground like snakes.
By their twos they come again
the motley herd of all creation
running the gauntlet of time
The compact of Noah is broken
the most ancient act of all the world
and beasts have souls.

The successors of morning
found the graph
of another planet's hell.

A city gaped
like the mouth of a suicide
where one lone angel
silently buried the dead.

Dresden was a carcass,
and it stank.
Dresden was a stone,
and it was shattered.
Dresden was a riddle
and we came to read it,
we,
the successors of morning.

STEALING FIGS

It's early August
a few years ago.
You are still alive.
The figs are ripe again.
I rise from our siesta.
The heat's tempered,
the shadows begin
their crawl toward night.
I take the broken road
and walk deep
into the country
past the pines and cypress
and the great hospital
on the hill.
Dogs bark
behind their fences
but the fig trees
lean out their new wealth.
I fill my pockets
each green succulence
swelling them
like an adolescent's balls.

It is dark when I get home.
I spread the haul for you
and you pounce on it
as eager as Eve
for the fruit of a forbidden tree
aflush with pleasure.

Your eyes are the first stars
of the night
and I am proud as any Adam.

ANNIVERSARY

I'm seeing you again
on the sunlit bench
where two men
fight over you.
The three of you
make a frieze
something
from a drama
a bit overdone.

I hesitate to join
then your eyes
are on me,
and all else
will be too late.
And if I hadn't
come down the few steps
of the famous library
on that day?
Destiny's a joke,
we are atoms colliding
and the whole story
of life on a minor planet
had no other purpose
but this: finding you.

The story's finished.
Time can run backwards
if it chooses
we can be forgotten
the cells of a brain
dissolving, the walls
of a heart collapsed.
It's a rarity
to meet on the moon.
Still, somewhere,
two lovers wait again
for their hour.

IN THE FIELD

In the field
blood was shed.
God stood by,
knowing why.
The mortal flow
sourceless now
spreads on the plain
seeps to the gate.
We ply the red lake
in the silent surround
heedless of the stain
blameless in the hour.
In the field
blood was shed.
God stood by,
knowing why.

HOW DID WE GET HERE?

A Conversation with *SVJ*'s New Poetry Co-Editors, Jane Edna Mohler and Mary Jo LoBello Jerome

Jane and I are editing the poetry section together, stepping into the spot more than 30 years after SVJ began. It's an honor to follow Bernadette McBride, Bill Wunder, and so many other brilliant poets who cultivated the SVJ poetry pages for years. Many thanks for this opportunity go to Peter Krok, SVJ Editor-in-Chief since 2001 and stalwart supporter of the arts.

But how did Jane and I get here? We had a conversation recently about our partnership and stewardship of the journal's commitment to bring the best poetry to the region. As poets and editors, of course we smoothed and abbreviated the discussion. We could go on for days, but instead we'll briefly introduce ourselves and share a bit of our aesthetic.

Mary Jo: I'll start. I've always been a poet—since a teenager. Ah. Those angsty teenage poems! You too, right?

Jane: Actually, I started in elementary school. My fourth-grade teacher, Mrs. Robinson, was excited about my writing. I never forgot what that meant to me.

Mary Jo: In my career, I've been a reporter, a writer and editor in various fields, and a teacher and assistant professor. I've published and studied fiction, but I've always come back to poetry. The beauty and power of words in a well-wrought poem can fill me, echo in me for days. I'm so ready to do this fun and fulfilling job, a perfect fit for my interests and energy right now. What are your thoughts on being an editor?

Jane: I was a counselor in various mental health settings for over thirty years. I was a poet first and I believe my poet mind informed my counseling practice. Now, as an editor I have a different awareness. I'm reminded that a novel concept is not enough to make a poem. A good poem needs originality *and* careful editing. Being an editor is sharpening my own poems.

Mary Jo: Absolutely. A poem really comes alive in revision. It's obvious when a poet has carefully crafted their work—word choice, the sound and rhythm of the lines, original metaphors, tight construction. A good poem shows something different, something that changes the way I think.

Jane: And that's what I look for in submissions. Surprises. Textured syntax, original connections, poems that make me sit up and consider something in a new way. I want a voice that is personal yet doesn't forget the rest of the world. Invite me into your perspective while you remember the reader and the world at large. You may be a *hero* in your poem, but the reader wants in on the deal.

Mary Jo: What have you been reading lately? Who are favorite poets or inspirations?

Jane: Most recently I've been reading Ada Limón's *Bright Dead Things*. I love her intimate voice. I'm taken with the "Asian Figures" in W.S. Merwin's collection of translations, *East Window*. Merwin describes the Figures as brief, "irreducible and unchangeable." Now that's a writing goal! And I always go back to the grounded voice of Charles Simic.

Mary Jo: I love Ada Limón, too. I just got her newest book. Right now, I'm reading and floored by "Post Colonial Love Poems" by Natalie Diaz. Ocean Vuong's "Time is a Mother" is next on my list. I always find so much in Mark Doty, Tony Hoagland, Ellen Bass, Ross Gay. But my desert island poets are Linda Pastan, Sharon Olds and William Carlos Williams. What about other creative pursuits that might find ways into your poems?

Jane: I belong to an American Traditional Rug Hooking guild. We make mats and rugs with wool strips cut from clothing collected at thrift stores. Fiber arts enable me to get outside of my word-mind but then, often they take me back to poetry. I could fill five lifetimes and still not get to all I have planned. As a child I played organ, blasting Bach before my feet could properly reach the pedals. I always wanted to return to keyboards and study piano. Hasn't happened yet, but it will.

Mary Jo: I keep my hands in the dirt. I garden and fight the snails and slugs. There's a fox family that's been visiting our yard regularly—I planted a bunch of biennial foxgloves for them this spring—and I've been writing about them. I want to make a chapbook of foxy poems with photos or illustrations. It will be a fun project.

Jane: Ha! Foxgloves. Sounds like we both spend lots of time at home, especially these past years. What other places lurk in your memories? For me, I have a soft spot for Asia, especially China. I taught English language camp for two summers at a university in Guangzhou. What a feeling to be in a place where I could barely communicate without English. I loved the marketplace: the sights, smells, sounds. I made lots of friends with the vendors and their kids. Smiles worked. I treasured the feeling of anonymity that I had there.

Mary Jo: I know what you mean. Being an outsider gives you the space to feel and see so much, to witness. I was lucky to live and work in Rotterdam and Tokyo for years. I remember distinctly the feeling of always being awake and alert. Nothing on autopilot. Especially in Japan, where every little thing was a discovery—not only the places and people but the simplest tasks, grocery shopping, riding the metro. I believe art arises from witnessing. To be open to witness is a gift for an artist, no matter what one sees or where.

Jane: Yes! A gift for anyone who keeps on the lookout for the creaks and crannies of different lives. Those resonant details, to borrow a phrase from the poet Chris Bursk, are the multivitamins for poems. I think it's very important too for our poems to hold a generous spirit. There's the art! I believe we send our poems out into the world as gifts the reader wants to open. I look forward to wrapping up more issues with you, Mary Jo.

Jessica de Koninck

THE BLESSINGS

It begins when I misread the title
of the meditation *as morning blessings*
with lesser names,

rather than *lesser-known names,*
for God. The service leader emphasizes
two of these: *rock of ages,*

fountain of living waters, and highlights
the places they appear in the text, but I am lost
in the lowlier—paper and scissors,
dry cell battery, cinder block.

Everything stands for something else,
that is to say; metaphor, and I get
more distracted from the meditation

and start thinking about Einstein who posited
that *God does not play dice with the Universe.*
I once agreed, but luck's so often a flashlight

that doesn't work when the power
goes out. Each night before bed
I try to remember to write three good things,

however small, about my day. Late night rain
watered the lawn. Peaches at the farmer's
market. Clean sheets on the bed.

Joseph Chelius

WALKING LAKE CAROLINE

With the coffee shops closed,
and the great pandemic
having set up its yellow barriers—
banning community
even at the community park—
I walk to the lake
just blocks from my house,
learning in these early hours
and after years of driving by
what the men in the reeds
have come to fish for:
perch and bluegill, smallmouth bass.

To listen while wending goose poop
along an asphalt trail
to the falls of the dam
and to a symphony of crickets
as they saw on their instruments;
discern at a foot bridge
what the local poets have inscribed
if not for the ages,
then at least through sophomore year:
Rat loves BB! Nat is bad!

To recognize at an overlooked place
the delight of nature in cobbling words:
loosestrife, milkweed, stubbly cat-o-nine-tails
someone described on Facebook
as a swath of corndogs bobbing on sticks.

And which the Lenape discovered
to be perfectly edible, their roastable tips
perhaps the very first junk food
as they settled to their night's viewing—
a people without a cable bill,
sharing the same screen,
gazing at the moon and stars
in those earliest days of public TV.

Michael J. Carter

THE HOUND OF SPRING

Birdie, a scent hound,
is trying to reinvent herself
as a smell hound
enthusiastically
perfuming her neck
with some dead thing
mucky under a pine tree.
Chilly spring morning,
perfect for sap, but not
for February, over
a month early. Under
a previous weather pattern
this meadow would be
in a deep freeze, more snow
than not, and yonder ponds
frozen for skating.
Evenings I look for comfort,
but rarely find any
and today add *bathe dogs*
to my list of chores
uncertain to be done.

Andrew Vogel

BLINDS

Cresting day, light falling along a mug and spilling pages,
the blankness that suspends, the print reaches outward.
Open blinds, we mind ourselves, hidden up inside sun-glaze.
Street trees and the odd walkers tap at our peripheries, all
coming to go, the view over the yards from the sink resolving
while a sauce stomps in its pot and the oven builds an idea,
our book broken on the counter, news talk and rumor on the air,
the exposures, the disclosures, the radiator patter stirring
an appetite, the puzzle piece telling us now where it belongs

as we never see the day and our hopes for it turning inward,
the brick street and walk, the rangy yew and stoop blossom
becoming the lamp on its stand, the pots swinging, dishes piled,
cupboards open, wine glass expiring, screen flaring, the sprawl,
the clutter of our accumulating failures shining bright for any
passerby to reckon, and if we stand just right all our reflections
can join with the neighbors over the way who are dancing
madly, as if for their lives, in their perfect little dining room.

Kurt Olsson

LA VIDA LOCA

Everyone in the room, even the cats, everyone in the house,
on the street, in the neighborhood, even in the sky, all asleep.

How wonderful to wake and take a long, deep breath
and fall back to sleep to this thought. And maybe, as you try

to doze off, take it a step further: there's a tiny principality
someplace, tucked behind a mountain pass perhaps, where

citizens sleep a sleep charmed and the dreams they dream
are like booths at a country fair and one can amble about

and touch and taste the wares—fresh-baked rhubarb pie,
apples still stamped by hoarfrost, a wedge of cheddar lovingly

carved in the shape of a fire truck, booties crocheted for
those with the native wit to wait until after tea to be born.

Ann Howells

TIME, TIDE, AND MOST OF A MOON

There must be a moment or two
in every life
that becomes a painting by Vermeer,
intimate glimpse into a life
somewhere near a river
or at the edge of a forest.

Dark curl clings to your forehead.
Egyptian cotton. Crazy quilt.
Mason jar filled with daffodils.

Walls are pale grey, chair arms worn,
quilts folded neatly on a shelf.
The moment hangs in a frame:
your tiny frown, my trembling lip,
wash of red-tinged sunset.
(It is easy to disappoint the young,
who expect so much.)

Past dissolves into present.
That friendly black dog—long gone.
Still, smell of pine, salt air.
Cottage, updated now, refurbished,
skylight admitting a new sun,
loft aglow, wedding ring quilt
an irony.

Plates of cheeses on a wobbly table.
Paper napkin. Stemmed glass.
Both chairs empty.

At dusk, tires crunch on gravel.
Moths swarm the porch light,
make it shimmer as though underwater.
I imagine I can hear them sizzle,
smell their flaming wings.

Lavinia Kumar

WOMAN ALTERING

Lava slowly flows
red
turns to stone

Words
force
over smiling lips

Her face slips
beyond
a two-way glass

Hot brandy
nectarine sips
whisper the throat

Once
a fruit tree
with blossoms

In slow motion
the flower
opened for a bird

Deborah Bayer

RED GOWN WITH LACE

As always, I'm drawn to this room, the one with the Chagalls,
but today, I'm not here for them. I came for this hard bench

under these dim lights to write about my mother. When I last
saw her, she listed hard to her left side, toward the port-wine

stain on her cheek, vivid on her pale skin. At my bedtime,
she often recounted the tale of her christening, how, instead

of making the sign of the cross on her forehead with holy water,
someone spilled a bottle of red wine over her white lace dress.

It was a soggy, ruined mess. Chagall's bride wears a long red gown
with lace edging at the neck and cuffs, covered by a long white veil.

The bride has pale hands.
        (One is flesh-toned, one is white.)
A fish leaps up to a red table.
        (His left hand holds a yellow-flamed candle.)
The groom holds his bride with yellow hands.

I thought the christening story was true. It puzzles me that my mother
leans to her left side. Her right side has failed her. Her speech is gone.

Expressive aphasia, the doctor said, *but she understands everything*.
On my mother's bird's-eye maple desk, the grain, still visible, is yellow

and dark. As a new wife, she rubbed linseed oil on it every week with
a soft cloth. Now she drags her left hand across an alphabet board.

Everything blurs as I look down at my notebook, up
at the paintings. Cerulean blue ink makes faint rings.

A man with a round blue head plays a recorder.
        (It's hard to see his hands.)
The bride and groom are surrounded by flowers.
        (A goat plays a green viola.)

The bride and groom float overhead in the dark blue air.

Katharyn Howd Machan

UNDER A SKY TOO MOLTEN TO BRUISE

The painter pauses.
What color from the palette?
What width brush?

Her daughter left again today
and this time maybe won't return.
How many miles between?

Fast clouds, far clouds
moving towards the easel
propped on leaf-strewn stones.

Which blue? Which gray?
Perhaps the purple of a thumbprint
where canvas shrieks its white.

after Jack Vian

Devon Miller-Duggan

PRAYER FOR BOYS IN 1914
THAT BECOMES A DIFFERENT SUPPLICATION

This was Then: every boy learnt the words of Horace.
And girls taught to never tell young men or fathers not
to go. Obedient.
They all learned wings, gas, wire, mud, and drowning.
They learned to fear the sky, the night. Forgive them.

Fire and shards of everything fell and rose.
Girls took to machines, and learned
the art of shells for fire and shards. Forgive.

The winged boys fed obedience and sweetness
saw crucifixion by barbed wire, infants thrown
into machines, woman's body after woman's body turned
into a field of grain, gleaned and tilled.

The proper boys all fell, as men will fall
improperly. They learned obedience of sitting,
of taking bitter on their tongues
and saying "sweet," of gun-burnt hands called "proper." Called
human. The Old War never stopped. Forgive:
Unteach children the fire-taste of blood.

Alan Perry

ENCROACHMENT

Yellow cactus flowers strike
a welcoming pose, petals
outstretched to greet
a smoky sun. But gray surrounds
the pot, darkens the ground
with ash, tiny cinders
like charcoal bits on a beach.

We wanted neighboring mesquite
and spiky blooms for our remote home
in the desert—far from traffic,
buildings, hydrants. But the air,
now nearly on fire in its own storm,
threatens the driveway, overrunning
our makeshift fire-break of dirt.

As I throw our go-bag in the truck,
the sky explodes to glower at us,
inflamed by our departure.
In the rearview mirror,
nothing left but an empty hose
extended near the flower pot,
another snake seeking water.

Lynne Viti

TWO STONE HEADS ON A BED OF THYME

Lying flat in a garden flanked by viburnum
a stone head purses its lips in a half-smile
mocking or laughing—I can't be sure.

Its comrade resembles
a sci-fi alien with bald ovoid head
goggle-eyes slanting downward in a V—
a Roman nose, nostrils flared
the mouth an O of surprise—or dismay.

Like us, these two awaken from isolation
after a spring, a summer, a winter
a second spring of discontent.
We ached to be with sons, daughters, parents.
We longed for the life we knew, the life
we wished to return to, that we feared was gone.
That may be gone.

Are we serene, wearing full-lipped smiles
or do our mouths form perfect circles of surprise?
Surrounded by abundant green, are we shocked or ecstatic
to be raised as if from the dead, this hot midsummer day?

Paul Ilechko

PIGEONS IGNORE A PRESENCE

Rock doves simper on the fence
   this garden is so much larger than
it used to be   while the town
is so much smaller   they are such strange
birds   evoking wisdom and stupidity
in equal measure   but soon the garden
will be buried beneath a foot
or more of snow   and the gaudy
starlings will assume control
                     beyond
the wall my father built from
generationally blackened stone
I sense the presence of an old friend
dead for many years   he wears
a velvet jacket and zippered boots
headphones clamp his greasy hair
   as a child I worshipped his sister
but their family was too rich
for us   my father a mere railwayman
   still   there were times we danced
together   her closeness electrifying
me   even more than the current
hovering of her brother's ghost.

Jane Rosenberg LaForge

LARGESS

My father lived off the largess
of bud, branch, and breath that reached
into the firmament, where it might
have been better welcomed
than on the lips he tried to read
to compensate for his deafness.
On his own he sought the cinnamon
he said would ease his diabetes;
as a child he chewed on sticks
like some tough guy with a cigar,
a stevedore or a gangster; as an adult,
he sprinkled it in his tea, though
it had no effect on his vitals.
If the pressure pricked high,
his sugar drilled low, and vice
versa; he sumptuously kept
a record of every blip, gasp,
and hiccup of his functions
and fortune, what made him
rich in the abstract, or doomed
for the inevitable wet blanket
that extinguished net and gross.
He often made a great exhibit
of his yellow legal pads but it was
the underside of the paper that
was more informative, a vascular map
wrought by the force he applied
to the pen onto paper, as if he meant
to carve an apology to my mother,
a rare act of remorse. She was

the accountant in the family, said
she'd show him how to cheat
on the taxes so he could better
keep his half but he refused
because he was committed
to failure, as a scholar depends
on the footnotes. At the bottom
of each page, he left the date,
time, and his signature, as if he had
created a work of art, a portrait
of all his achievements and what
nourished him, out of someone
else's deficits.

Koss

TELEMOTHER

The telephone rings and I pick up
       you say nothing but your vacuous womb thrums

in the phone line   your hara   your still point   ours
       we are connecting . . . the mother/daughter way . . .

forever bound in the pre-tongued void because
       you birthed me in an accidental winter

we are hitched with an invisible umbilicus
       I feel your tang in the silence

"Hello, hello," not a word
       but I know it's you I sit in

your stillness as my stomach wrings itself
       dry, stare at the wall

feeling your hollow and stay there
       until the quivering creep of your God clambers

up my spine and head then I shiver and hang up
       Jesus washed you white as snow you told me once or more

You say your bible repels demons You take it everywhere—
       just in case You get a lot of demon attention

at 7-11   the post office   the bus stop Thank goodness
       for bibles   fast reflexes and the adeptness of printing presses

An ordinary day could otherwise be an Armageddon
       And thanks lord for the convenience of telephones

with their curly umbilici and apt plugs
       and receivers that hang up

So many things to be grateful for
       It's cold outside December and it's just starting to snow

Jesus brings a gentle washing even to sinners
       like me in Ann Arbor on a strangely quiet Saturday

Jessica de Koninck

DRIFTING

I dreamed Paul was pushing
a supermarket shopping cart
along a concrete city sidewalk.
The cart haphazardly stacked
and filled with tools and electronic
gadgets. Although he wore a buttoned
shirt, I thought he looked like someone
homeless and woke to that image,
thinking death is its own kind
of homelessness.

The idea took root, perhaps,
at the evening's meeting when parents
complained about the vagrant
who muttered loudly to the children
walking home after Hebrew school.
The adults thought the security guard
should have done something. We spend
so much money on safety. I don't know.

Paul, in the dream, had rolled
his white sleeves to the elbow. I picture
him whistling, wheeling his possessions
along the empty sidewalk, the metallic
cart vibrating on uneven pavement.
It held so many chisels, screwdrivers,
wrenches. What did he plan to fix?

Devon Miller-Duggan

MARY EXPLAINS SOME THINGS TO THE SOUTHERN BAPTIST CONVENTION VIA PARABLE

There is a hospital on the other side—
say "Mental Hospital" or "Sanitarium" or "Mad House."
Call it "Asylum" without irony—
all the patients women,
all found their way after rape,
all found unbearable by families and streets.

Half the patients can't or will not eat,
half eat everything to evolve walls, carapaces, sarcophagi.
All say *He raped me.*
Say it, say it to each other. Sometimes it means
"You lived another night. Welcome."
Sometimes, "I was loved, then I was food."
Some, "I was a child. I am still. I do not understand."
Some, "Please eat today; just a spoonful."

They sort rags by color all day.
They beat emptied cans into crosses incised with birds.
They rock for hours.

In this hospital, all doctors are male
and speak only of God, always in the passive.
Every patient owns a mustard seed—
some carried in their bodies,
some bound in their hair,
some secreted beneath thin pillows.
All the women dream they are trees.
All dream they are axes.

Marisa P. Clark

NECKLACE

She looms close, unbuttons her shirt,
peels back the collar to show the chain
of tumors like lurid baubles strung
across her chest. She says they're shrinking,
don't I think? They look like insect stings
magnified. Hot pink pustules, boils,
blisters from bad burns. Could a poke
from a needle pop them, let the injury
ooze out? Could they rupture? Do they
weep? If I pressed one with my fingertip,
would it shift like a cushy throw pillow
to accommodate a weary head? I know
better than to press, but I'm dumb enough
to ask what they feel like, if they hurt.
She doesn't touch to check. They're hard,
she says, and yes, constantly. She pinches
her collar shut and buttons up to hide
the necklace I didn't ask to see.

Keith Kopka

YOU TELL ME A CHILD IS NOT A PART OF YOUR PLAN

and I find myself nodding in agreement.
Because who doesn't feel comfort
when some sense of order emerges? A twinge
of peace when the geese return
each spring. The expected is not without beauty,
but attraction is often complicated by desire
to control what comes next. Each new day, an unopened
envelope held up to the light of the one
before it. It's scientific fact. Geese migrate
because of competition for food, but popular opinion
favors these birds fly hundreds of miles
to enjoy the weather their homecoming signals.
To be selfish, by definition, is to concentrate on one's
own advantage without regard for others.
There's a legend of a Persian king
who, after winning a great battle, looked out
over the retreating Greek army then charged his servant
to warn him three times daily:
"Master, remember the Athenians." He knew the war
wasn't over, that his enemies' willingness
to return another time was not a gesture of attrition.
Geese honk across the sky. Do you hear them?
Their Doppler like a chorus of broken clown horns.
A young boy crouches in a blind listening
to his father's instructions. *Never aim at the bird.*
Instead, aim where the bird is about to be.
His hands bake like sauna rocks in his thick hunting gloves.
He knows they're needed to keep his skin
from barrel burns, but he still wants to take them off.
My love, I agree with your reasoning
but not your reason. The Greeks defeated the Persian army
at the battle of Marathon. Convinced he'd burn
Athens to the ground, that same king
sent an invading force before the Greeks could return
to his shores. The geese are circling.
If you shoot at an empty space, you will never miss.

Michael J. Carter

THE POPPIES

own teaching
on impermanence
is lost
on them
leaping each
year into
the wild
air with
adolescent abandon
untouchable, inviolate
brassy with
pheromonal confidence.
They'll never
know what
hit them,
it is
already too
late.

Andrew Vogel

ABYME

Here a summer of fireflies,

pirouetting zeppelins, clumsily
surfing an evening's blue drafts,
gleaming their intermittent beacons.

They sleep all day, granting mornings
to the crickets with their timid racket,
ceding afternoons to the fat cicadas,

dreaming all the while of falling stars,
but come twilight, they crowd this little
fenced plot with their ticklish orbits.

The neighbor's tabby and I gaze

curious abstraction as they zoom
the stout begonias, the blooming
hosta fronds, the lilies coming on.

The violence is entirely inside us.

Our potted herbs gulp the humidity
while they ping, flickering constellations,
as if our patio garden were a universe

absolute unto itself, and I never
want to step outside that gate
and risk thinking otherwise.

Joe Benevento

I HIT A SQUIRREL WITH A CHILD'S GREEN PLASTIC WATERING CAN

From my deck to the feeder below, fifteen feet away,
knocking him off his precarious perch and onto the green
grass blackened by the remains of myriad sunflower seeds.

If I were hit by an unnatural green missile I think I'd run,
maybe to the wide red cedar where he and all his rodent
and avian fellow feeders usually seek cover.

He just stands my ground, though, not dazed nor hurt,
with a calm, dark gaze that seems to say, "Is that all you
got, old man?"

I've been chasing squirrels off a dozen times a day
with everyone else in the household wondering
why I would bother.

They keep the birds I want to see away: the rose-
breasted grosbeaks, the goldfinch, the cardinals
all keep their colors to themselves, in fear of fox and gray squirrels.

If I were a hunter I guess they would be easy prey,
but I'm not and they know it, so they keep coming back
no matter how far off the deck I run or what I might heave from it.

My only consolation, the accuracy of that one toss, though even
that feels more like a carnival trick, the one where you knock down
all the pins but receive some crummy prize

from the squirrely guy in charge
laughing to himself about having
fleeced yet one more fool.

Lynda Gene Rymond

WHERE ART THOU, MERRIMENT?

I cannot remember
the last time you tripped along
with your broken-in hat,
whistling through your teeth
even as you sharpened time's scythe.
Crap, yes, life is hard,
that's why there's lemon meringue pie,
Fats Waller, and nightcrawlers.

Now we have Joy
and her suitcases of spiritual significance,
lugubrious Mindfulness, who won't touch
dairy, and Affirmation,
who keeps her puppy in a crate.

I haven't guffawed since the Internet,
when Merriment fashioned a bindlestiff,
took off on a one laner
looking for a place with hollyhocks hiding
a two-holer outhouse.

Here am I holding a bandana.
I could stitch yet another covid mask
or roll up a couple cans sardines,
a box of saltines, an apple,
tie it all to a stick and head out,

tracking Merriment
like a beagle
with velvet ears and bugle cry
following the scent
of teaberry gum.

John Wojtowicz

BRING YOUR TRACTOR TO CHURCH SUNDAY

In the gravel lot, generations
of Massey-Fergusons
and Allis-Chalmers. Chases
and Fords. John Deeres
and Farmalls muse about weather.
Most of the congregation
haven't seen each other
since the last holiday
but not much has changed,
a few old-timers succumbed to rust;
their farms parceled
into postage stamps. Others
retired to front lawns like milk bottles
on windowsills. A sermon
for the harvest and hymns
about sowing seeds
echo from sandstone walls,
sung by men in unstained overalls.
Only a handful still swagger
on mud-covered ag tires,
proud as quarter horses, resolved
to keep their pastures
from sprouting housing complexes.

Jo Angela Edwins

THE WHITE SPIDER

living in my yard on wild honeysuckle vine
tried to hide from me. It didn't succeed.
How most everything of a weaker breed
knows to run from the stronger is perhaps a sign
of—what? Evolution? Intelligent design?
Of a sudden I wondered what creatures bleed
the palest of blood, and if their need
of that blood is the lesser for it. The shine
of August sun on the spider made it seem
a ghost of itself, translucent, a shawl
of spindly gauze caught on a petal, the gleam
of dew on its thorax like tears on cream.
I let it live, although great nature kills us all
in time, no matter how well hidden, how small.

Alan Perry

CYCLES

The washing machine hisses as it sprays
water over soiled laundry, mixing soap

I poured in the tub–food to fuel its work.
The cylinder surges as fabrics lilt up and down,

gently pulsing dirt out of clothes
down the drain, like the way we shed

our epithelia, bits and flakes at a time,
re-inventing skin that gives way to pink again.

As the cleansing nears completion,
the machine rumbles, bangs

against the wall, thumps on the floor.
Damp clothes begin their wind down, spinning

in a force that keeps them pressed together.
The sequence ended, I notice sheets

wrap themselves around everything,
like legs entwined in bed, clinging tighter

than skin on skin, silk to satin.
I gently peel apart the cottons and linens,

my pant leg knotted around a blouse–
her bra entwined with my shirt so firmly

they look inseparable. But they're not.
Delicate things need to breathe.

John Reed

YOUR NAME WAS WRITTEN ALL OVER ME

We were there on the street corner,
standing too close together, or too far apart,
and your name was written all over me,
in fat marker, chisel-tip, red and black.
Oh, and all caps. Name, first and last, and times
and dates, and percentages, usually
quite high, like eighty-eight or ninety-four.
The red ink had wept onto my collar.
And that friend of yours, or maybe mine,
looked from you to me, and from me to you,
while we acted like sorta acquaintances,
and made introductions, casually,
until—whose friend?—ran off to not see more.

John Reed

AND THEN

And then you were a fuzzywuzzy bunny.
And then you were a three-sided dagger.
And then you were a torn flag on a flagpole.
And then you were happy hour and nylons.
And then you were me, and then you were you.
And then you were a shack by a mountain.
And then you were a Billy Idol song.
And then you were Ziggy, then Jewel.
And then you were a June day with no fan.
And then you were money honey money.
And then you were a street and a stranger.
And then you were a red-check duffle coat.
And then you were here, and then you were gone.

Lynda Gene Rymond

MYSTERY MAN

Every seventh day that winter,
he drove an old white van
covered with hand-lettered bible verses

to a stretch of backroad
between two dessicated cornfields,
under transmission towers that sizzled in the damp.

Wary of zealots,
I'd wait for him to leave
before taking my dog Reba to the fieldbreak.

When we walked down Silo Hill
toward Anna's farmhouse,
his flowers edged the road.

He'd planted cut long-stemmed red roses
into frozen roadside dirt
where they, of course, died standing and rootless.

Next week, another section of roses jammed
beside their dying cousins
who were alongside those quite dead.

My curiosity and I knocked on Anna's door,
sipped boiled black coffee with sugar
not too near the crackling pot-belly stove.

"Heaven knows!" laughed the old Mennonite.
"He's said not a peep to us. He plants those roses,
waters them, prays to the four directions and goes."

Then, the fresh roses stopped appearing. The van
gone, the small brown-skinned man gone,
the sign he hoped for, I suppose, a "no."

But then, I suppose too much,
being spectator without a program
to explain this Play of Mysteries.

Bruce McRae

FROM A FROZEN PLANET

I remember a wedding on Fornax.
The juices of Cepheus.
A girlish sneeze in the Virgo cluster.

I remember every third star was bent
on getting home before dawn.
The smudged thumb of the universe.
A calm in the eye of the mind's storm.

It was warm for midnight,
the gods' dog, Sirius, snarling,
asteroids taking their star turns,
dark matter spangling the ozone.

Light kicked holes in night's imperfections
and the candy-canes of Sagittarius.
Red-headed Mars was over the moon,
Neptune cradled in a willow's arms,
being gently soothed, rocking back
and forth to the music of Time.

I remember a cosmic spider and galactic web.
The carbon dunes in Perseus.
Mispronouncing, twice, Iapetus.

I recall a night so quiet
you could hear the planets thinking
and a sulphur-slide on a faraway world.
I remember a last gamma-ray
before daylight barged in,
before morning's boast and courage,
before the sun's brash glory
overshadowed everything, the something
which was nothing, but wasn't.

Kelly R. Samuels

LONGING FOR ST. KILDA

We will need ginger on this trip—
      for the rise and plummet, the slap
and spray.

Favorable weather conditions mean more. Mean *wind speed*
and *sea swell* alongside a stretch of clear hours.

      For it's an island we're after.

    The lone. The contained.

      The drop, forming

like mercury.

There are no trees to climb, but cliffs—for the bird
and the egg. And he'll tell us of how the man fell.
How the child fell.

So I'll walk where it's flat. Note the cleits and ruins
and moss. Pocket a stone to set on the window
ledge hours later, far from.

Wendy Fulton Steginsky

URSULA JUST WANTS TO WEAR SASS

Ursula thought she was named for a little bear
but in reality it's one of the mighty Gorgon sisters
who growled like a beast and proved immortal.

Ursula definitely fancies the idea of immortality
and wings, which artists bestowed on the sisters
wreathing antique pots and sculpted in marble.

Adept at staring people down,
Ursula thrills at the idea of Medusa's gaze
turning her enemies into stone. Secretly,

she makes a list and errs on the side of plenty.
Then she contemplates twirling her head
of venomous snakes at one or two of them.

***

When an octopus dreams, it turns Technicolor:
white to yellow, flashes vermilion, then mottled green
and twitches like a dog chasing squirrels in its mind.

After discovering this, Ursula fashions a dream catcher
of multiple interlocking coils that can dangle
as sea foam and violet arms above her bed.

Octopuses (not octopi) have nine brains, three hearts
and blue blood. Imagine: behind her lids, multiple brains
to plot grand schemes; beneath her breast, three hearts

for greater stamina, and coursing through
her arteries, the blue blood of nobility.
Ursula has always known she is imperious.

Now she's completely sold on her kinship
with an octopus. She can't believe there's anything
more she'd desire, except to wear its sass.

John Wojtowicz

COPING MECHANISMS

My 5-year-old daughter sulks in the bathroom

because my gingerbread man
arrived at Candyland before hers did.

I approach with empathetic intentions
for some new-fashioned progressive parenting.

But, in-between sobs, I can hear the sounds
of her imitating a chicken.

Sob. Bawk. Sob-Sob. Bawk-Bawk. Sob.

I step away from the door. Her mother isn't home
and this one wasn't in the book.

Sniffle. Cluck. Sniffle. Cluck. Sniffle. Cluck-Cluck.

I have a vision of her sprouting feathers
and acknowledge I'm going to have to knock.

Squawk-Squawk. Giggle-Giggle. Squawk. Flush.

When I reluctantly ask about the chicken
sounds, she makes beaks with her hands,

flaps her elbows, and twists to the tempo
of make-believe accordion music.

She tells me that sometimes when she has a sad thought
she makes a chicken noise.

Another sad thought, another chicken noise
until she's laughing instead of crying.

*Holy-Zen-mother-of-mindfulness-coping-
mechanisms-for-emotional-regulation.*

And you might have one or three
of these little bodhisattvas at your house.

Mine yells: *Shake your tail feathers, Daddy!* And so, I do.

Robert Zaller

COURAGE AND THE COMMONS
IN POSTWAR AMERICAN FILM

Courage is the rarest of all virtues and yet the most universal, since we must all summon it at some time in our lives. War is the activity that most concentrates it, and the warrior is still among the most esteemed of cultural figures. As the poet Robinson Jeffers put it, uncomfortably but with an unmistakable ring of truth, "Stark violence is still the sire of all the world's values."[1]

The relationship between war and courage is at the same time the most paradoxical, for if war is the most organized of human activities, courage is also the most individual. War breeds synonyms for it; we speak too of valor, and of bravery. Both of these terms may be applied to individuals, but also to more collective performance; 'valor' implies a continuity of enterprise, and 'bravery' is as often applied to fighting units as to the individuals who comprise them. It is courage, however, that is the irreducible core of these wider terms. You can order armies into battle; you cannot compel courage. How and why it appears is, at bottom, a mystery of the spirit.

It is similarly a mystery how courage relates not only to the specialized activity of warfare but to cultural construction as such—to the formation of community. The hero, who may or may not be a warrior, is the foundation of the social bond, and it is prowess even among primates that organizes the host. In more advanced human groupings this prowess need not be primarily physical, and in the most advanced, which we call civilizations, it is typically a religious founder who embodies the hero's role. But daring is never absent in the highest undertakings, and daring is never without courage.

Our greatest poets, Homer and Shakespeare, thought deeply on these subjects, and the greatest human conflict to date, the Second World War, produced a particularly troubled reflection of them. In America, it would permeate the new art form that had arisen chiefly between the two world wars and addressed the largest of mass audiences: film.

Mainstream Hollywood responded to Pearl Harbor by a call to arms and the sacrifice of a united nation. But, especially with the arrival of a displaced community of talented European writers and directors, films of a distinctly darker tone began to emerge in the 1940s. The genre acquired a name of its own, film noir, and its style and themes penetrated much of more serious filmmaking in the postwar era. It blended, too, with one of the most characteristic tropes of American culture, the relation between the lone individual and the formation of community.

The present essay will focus on three films that, spanning the McCarthy era and the course of the Cold War, examine this subject in contrasting ways. None of them speak directly to the events of their decade, but all are saturated by its climate. Two of them are the work of a single director, Fred Zinnemann, and two of them feature the same lead, Gary Cooper. Taken together, they probe deeply the relation of acts of courage, in war and out of it, to the communities they both constitute and challenge.

Zinnemann, a Jewish emigrant slowly working his way up the film industry of the 1930s, would lose both his parents in the Holocaust. The most distinctly noir film of his career, *Act of Violence,* had clear biographical resonances, and its theme would be not heroism but cowardice. Its protagonist, Frank Enley (Van Heflin), lives with the truth that he has betrayed the men under his command in a Nazi POW camp, only to be relentlessly pursued by a survivor, Joe Parkson (Robert Ryan). Enley's flight from Parkson in a chilling descent from a raucous trade convention to a prostitute's bed and an arrangement with a hired killer, evokes in a few clipped scenes a stark American underworld. Zinnemann's next film, *The Men,* focused on a paraplegic veteran, likewise dealt with the suppressed costs of war. But it was only with his *High Noon*—a Western in setting, but a Greek tragedy in form, the story of a man set against his *polis*—that we encounter a classic statement of our theme.

Like *Act of Violence, High Noon* is shot in black and white, the preferred, spectral style of film noir; but, unlike noir, its quality is harshly open and its narrative climax arrives at the one unshadowed moment of the day. Will Kane, the retiring marshal of Hadleyville, is marrying a young Quaker, Amy Fowler (Grace Kelly), and about to leave without ado on the noon train whose next day's run will bring his replacement. Kane is a respected but solitary figure who has pacified a frontier town, but put down no roots in it. If, as the town's shifty mayor (Thomas Mitchell) says, he has made Hadleyville safe to raise a family in, he will not bring his own up in it.

The casting of Gary Cooper as Will Kane has come to seem inevitable, not only for Cooper's iconic performance but for his previous roles, notably that of Sergeant Alvin York, America's most famous military hero. Those who declined the part were a Who's Who of Hollywood luminaries, including Marlon Brando, John Wayne, Gregory Peck, Charlton Heston, and Montgomery Clift. All of these performers, Wayne excepted, were youthful. Cooper, a weathered fifty, was the eldest of the group. As matters proved, his age was in many ways the defining element of the film, underscoring the precariousness of the order he represented.

Kane's planned departure is interrupted by sudden news of the return of Frank Miller (Ian McDonald), the town's former scourge and Kane's personal nemesis, who, awaited by confederates, is arriving on the very train Kane is scheduled to take.[2] Kane has few choices. With no further authority, he cannot safely remain in town; leaving it, he is a target on the open road. What brings him up short, however, is the thought of fleeing a moral responsibility. That others may think ill of this does not concern him, at least in the moment. It is rather what he will think of himself.

Kane returns to town alone, the pacifist Amy having refusing to accompany him. His former deputy, Harvey (Lloyd Bridges), has been left in charge until the new marshal's arrival; Kane has time, if only a little of it, to gather a posse.

The reception he will meet, at least from some, is indicated by the cynical clerk of the town's hotel (Howland Chamberlain) where Kane's former lover Helen (Katy Jurado) has her rooms, and her own reasons for departure as Miller's former mistress as well. This fact, as well as Helen's own reputation (she has run the town saloon), complicates our sense of who Kane is. The sheriff who's had his own brushes with the law is of course a trope of Western lore, but, although this is not overtly indicated here—indeed, Kane appears as an antithesis to the brutal and vicious Miller—their personal animosity is notorious. Both, with Miller's crimes pardoned, are moreover now civilians. Kane is the man leaving, and Miller the one returning. As the town had once belonged to the latter, so it might again.

It is a Sunday, and the town's respectable citizens are in church. The saloon, however, is open too, and doing brisk business in anticipation of the new dispensation. Kane returns to his office to pick up his badge and recruit his posse. Some reject or evade him from fear and cowardice; some from self-interest. Harvey demands that he support him for promotion. The town's judge, having gauged the temper of the town, is packing his law books when Kane approaches him. His own predecessor (Lon Chaney Jr.), aged and embittered, is too spent to be of use. Both he and the judge have only the same advice to give: that Kane escape while he can. His death, the judge tells him, will not even be an act of principle, but merely a pointless waste.

The climactic scene of Kane's futile quest comes when he appeals to the churchgoers, to whom he nakedly appeals for assistance. A debate ensues, with no common sentiment emerging. Finally the mayor intercedes, praising what Kane has done for Hadleyville but warning that all may be lost if bloodshed erupts. Kane's final service, he suggests, will be to preserve the peace, and with it the town's future, by quitting it.

The mayor's speech is met with a murmur of concurrence. Kane withdraws silently to meet what he now understands to be his fate, and, alone in his office, writes his will. Zinnemann pans the receding tracks of the train station where Miller's gang awaits him repeatedly, each time evoking not simply tension but impending doom. *High Noon* is conventionally viewed as a parable of the McCarthy era, and the interpretation is not inapt.[3] But the obsessiveness of the image suggests a deeper subtext, particularly in view of Zinnemann's personal history. The reference is finally clarified: it is to the image that most characteristically signifies the Holocaust, the narrowing tracks that approach the terminus of Auschwitz.

Hadleyville is not of course to be a site of genocide, but rather of moral abdication. For some, as we have seen, this will be not unwelcome, and vice a source of profit as well as pleasure. Kane himself is an ambiguous figure, but still, as Helen reminds us, "a man": not unflawed, not unfearful, but someone who does what he must when it must be done. As in *Act of Violence*, Zinnemann does not skirt the fallibilities of human nature. Evil, however, was a far more radical condition, and when Frank Miller does arrive, we confront it in no uncertain terms. If he enters an unresisting town, justice will have no place in it.

A last scene prefaces the dénouement. Harvey confronts Kane in the town stable, trying to force him to mount and leave. Unlike most of the town he appears unmotivated by fear, and in all likelihood he has calculated how he will make his truces with Miller. His problem will be Kane's martyrdom. The town will no doubt enfold his sins into their own, but, as the mayor has warned it of outside judgment if violence erupts, so Harvey realizes that he will be perceived as the Judas who has betrayed not only his office but the one man who upholds it. The Christological elements of the plot come to their climax here, and, if Kane prevails in the struggle with Harvey, the beating he takes in their fight leaves him all the more exposed to the men he must face.

Amy has meanwhile returned to town, partly shamed by Helen and partly by the realization of where her true devotion lies. She kills one of Miller's men who has Kane in his sights, and then, clawing free of Miller's grip, frees Kane for his own shot. The two stand together in the street as a crowd forms around them, but it is Kane on whom the focus tightens as the town is drawn to the only force that now binds it. Stiffening, Kane drops his badge into the dust, and swivels away. There is no need for more; all his contempt, the finality of his rejection of those he has served, is in the opening of a palm and the turn of a heel. It is one of the great gestures in film, and the moment belongs sublimely to Cooper.

Courage does not link or create community in *High Noon*; it attests its collapse. Like any effort at community, Hadleyville reflects the human compound; it is no better or worse than any other of its time or place, and the likes of Frank Miller will always find some degree of reception in it. The new marshal will arrive on the next day's train. He will hear the story it suits the town to tell—no doubt it will be the mayor who tells it—and not ask more questions than necessary. The badge will lie in the dust.

The second film we consider, *They Came to Cordura,* appeared at the end of the McCarthy era, with McCarthy himself disgraced and dead. Hollywood was nonetheless still deeply blighted by its effects. Robert Rossen, the film's director, had like other prominent Hollywood figures bowed to the pressure to name names after the blacklisting that followed inquisition by the House Unamerican Activities Committee. *They Came to Cordura,* too, would be a study in courage and betrayal.

Unlike Will Kane in *High Noon,* Major Thomas Thorn—again Gary Cooper, in his penultimate film role—is no hero but a self-described coward obsessed by the nature of courage. The moment that has damned him is the Battle of Columbus, when he had shirked combat in a retaliatory raid against an American border town by the Mexican revolutionary Pancho Villa. As the son of a general, Thorn's behavior is notorious although officially covered up. When the military pursues Villa into Mexico, Thorn is assigned to a cavalry regiment as an Awards Officer. The task is punitive, since it is both beneath his rank and a means of mockery, as his duty is to identify battlefield heroism.

Arreaga (Carlos Romero), a lieutenant of Villa's, has taken refuge with his men in the walled hacienda of an American woman, Adelaide Geary (Rita Hayworth). The colonel who leads the regiment, (Robert Keith), obsessed with winning glory for what he believes may be the last cavalry charge in the new era of modern warfare—it is 1916—storms the hacienda despite its heavy fortification. As the battle line is broken, individual soldiers launch attacks on foot, finally breaching the hacienda's gates. Arreaga retreats, leaving the regiment with its bloody victory and Adelaide to be taken captive. Thorn, meanwhile, cites four men for the valor that has turned the day.

Thorn rejects the colonel's demand for a citation for himself, privately appalled at the senseless loss of life for a secondary objective. The colonel threatens him with public exposure, but he stands his ground, a first act of courage that suggests a journey of redemption. With permission from the expedition's commander, he pulls the four troopers out of line to ensure their personal safety and the delivery of their commendations, with a fifth added from another company. This itself entails passage as a small mounted unit over unsecured ground to the forward base of Cordura. Adelaide, remanded for having given aid and comfort to the enemy, is added to the party. She objects, arguing that she had been forced to quarter Arreaga's men and pointing out that, since no adversary had been declared by Congress, no "enemy" officially existed.

The latter objection would have had particular resonance in the 1950s, when the United States fought a major war in Korea without Congressional authorization. The point would be underscored when Thorn noted that America's looming involvement in Europe's Great War would be bolstered by recognized acts of courage closer to home. Unspoken but clearly implied was that the brush war with Mexico would be a step toward executive fiat and thence to empire, and in fact its leader, John Pershing, would soon find himself in command of the American Expeditionary Forces in France.

Thorn himself, however, has a more personal reason for giving his group safe conduct. The men he has selected have all displayed the courage that, called to the test, he had lacked, and en route he prods them further to discover what has impelled them to act in battle, as he somewhat starchly puts it, "beyond the normal limit of human conduct." What Thorn is in actuality attempting is to constitute them as a community whose singular virtue makes of them a band of brothers and a company of the elect. Such a quality, if capturable, will do more than build ésprit. It will validate the military life. The engagement at the hacienda, poorly planned and desperately executed, had been, as Thorn privately confides, no more than a "farce." What redeemed it, what was capable of redeeming all battle as such, was the occasion it provided for courage, as what redeemed religious practice was the opportunity for the saintly act.

The latter point is driven home by Thorn's interview with the outsider in the group, Hetherington (Michael Callan), a sympathetic youth who broods on his loss of faith. Hetherington has little recollection of what he did in battle or why, but only, as he says, that at the critical moment his belief had been restored. The other men have little to humanly commend them, and, each having a personal reason to protect his anonymity, they reject their medals. The worst of the lot is Sergeant Chawk (Van Heflin), who threatens to reveal Thorn's cowardice if he is not allowed to have Adelaide. Matters worsen when they are surprised by Arreaga's retreating forces, who pin them down as they exhaust their few supplies. The treacherous ride to Cordura turned into a nightmare, Chawk reveals Thorn's secret, thus robbing him of all authority but bare rank. Adelaide suggests that Arreaga's men are uninterested in their party but only its horses. She is correct, but when Thorn turns the horses loose they are left to proceed themselves on foot. Now facing virtual mutiny, Thorn commands his next in rank, Lieutenant Fowler (Tab Hunter), to throw away all weapons but his own. To make matters worse, Hetherington falls ill of typhoid, forcing the others to carry him on a litter.

The litter breaks what little solidarity the men have. Burdened by a man unknown to them and believed (or hoped) to be dying, and with Cordura's location uncertain, they wish only to go their separate ways as quickly as they can. This, however, is impossible as long as Thorn himself lives. Chawk stalks him, threatening to kill him in his sleep. Thorn realizes that he cannot act against him, since this will only unite the rest of the men in rebellion. His only ally is Adelaide, who, with Thorn as her sole protector, keeps vigil beside him and, as he finally loses consciousness, gives herself to Chawk to distract him.

A break in fortune occurs when the party comes upon a rail line, and with it a handcar that enables them to dispense with the litter. The car requires two men to properly operate, but only one will join Thorn, who works now without respite as well as sleep. Finally only Adelaide assists him, and in the end he is reduced to dragging the car by rope alone. At this point, the men have their solution; Thorn's refusal to abandon Hetherington will bring about his own collapse and inevitable death. Fowler, joining the other mutineers, fells Thorn with a rock, and Adelaide is tripped up when she tries to aid him. As Thorn collapses at last, the men move off to watch him die. Only Adelaide, now a Magdalene-like figure, tells him he is the bravest man she has ever met.

Fowler, taking command, tells the men they will all agree on a story about Thorn's demise. Chawk, though, remembers the book in which Thorn has written not only their citations but his interviews with them. Without the book there can be no awards; and without it, too, any incriminating evidence Thorn may have recorded about them. It will be destroyed, of course; but the men, wanting to know its contents, demand that it be read aloud first.

It is Chawk who does so. Thorn's jottings make his progressive disenchant-ment with the men clear, but also the growth of his charity toward the weak-nesses and complexities of human character. The men have revealed them-selves as mercenary, often cruel, and sometimes vile. Despite this, however, each has had a moment of transcendence, and in that moment placed the lives of others above his own. There is, Thorn writes, a "crippled child" in all men; but he takes it upon himself to prove that "something else also lives in them."

Chawk is silenced by these words, as are the others. Adelaide sees life stir in Thorn, and attends him. Hetherington, from a rise, sees Cordura on the plain below. Fowler warns them that if Thorn lives they will face court-mar-tial. But the moment, at least, unites them, and with Thorn at their head, they proceed toward the town.

Thorn is a man disillusioned not only with himself but with the life that sur-rounds him in general. The battle at the hacienda had been fought to gratify a single man's vanity; the war it reflected was one country's meddling in the civil wars of another. Courage, then, was divorced from cause, and insofar as it had value it was solely in itself. What Thorn attempts to raise from this sordidness is a community not of the just but the brave, as if the supremely individual act of courage could itself be the bond of men. The result, until Thorn's own example at the end, is just the reverse: the men he has brought together neither value nor understand the act he perceives as uniting them, or bring it into any intelligible relation to themselves. Nor can he himself persuade them otherwise, since his motivation in exposing them to further danger, if they can understand it at all, seems merely the coward's abuse of command to punish them for what he himself does not possess.

It is only in Chawk's reading of the awards book that the men begin to glimpse Thorn's refusal to reject their humanity even as he yields his falsely idealized vision of them. His fault is to have elevated a momentary event as definitive; as Adelaide tells him, no single act whether of cowardice or courage can define the whole of a man. Rather, when she describes him as the bravest man she has known, she suggests to him the many small but determined acts by which he has attempted to recall the others to their duty, and insist upon it at no matter what cost to himself. It is such a duty, the one that Kane similarly appeals to in the citizens of Hadleyville, that maintains community, and it is one that all owe to themselves.

The film's resolution is problematic. As the men begin their descent to Cordura, little has been resolved: mutiny against a superior officer; attempted rape and the intended abandonment of a fellow soldier; incriminating admissions of misconduct and worse. Whatever higher compassion Thorn has found, it by no means follows that he is absolved of the duty to report derelictions: as Fowler has suggested, there will need to be a "story" to explain events, or to conceal them. The momentary unity of purpose, then—survival—will be no foundation of community.

The Glendon Swarthout novel on which *They Came to Cordura* was based had a bleaker ending, and Columbia Pictures insisted on one at least partly consoling. The film was, nonetheless, as dark a vision war as any of the period, and must of course be considered on its own terms. Courage, as exhibited in it, does not unify but isolates, as an experience fundamentally incommunicable. The only thing the men on Thorn's forced march share is the desire to escape the memory of an act in which they cannot recognize themselves and which they do not wish to recall. Thorn attempts to make of courage not only a ground of community but a species of sanctity. But, although men in battle sometimes save, they more often kill.

In the dozen years after *High Noon,* Fred Zinnemann directed a variety of successful films, ranging from *From Here to Eternity* to *The Nun's Story.* He then returned to the theme of *High Noon,* but with his lens angle reversed. *Behold a Pale Horse*—the title, famously, taken from Revelation 6.8, depicting the opening of the Fourth Seal that looses Death on the world astride a horse[5]—depicts Manuel Artiguez (Gregory Peck), an exiled veteran of the

Spanish Civil War who returns to his native town of San Martín each year to offer a resistance to the Franco regime now effectively reduced to himself and a single, superannuated comrade, Pedro (Paolo Stoppa). Artiguez too is past his prime, and his will now flags in a cause largely forgotten or at least buried for his fellow countrymen. If, however, he no longer seems very alive for himself, he is very much so to his antagonist, Captain Viñolas of the fascist *Guardia Civil* (Anthony Quinn), whose failure to capture Artiguez is a perennial source of personal frustration and professional humiliation.

The impending death of Artiguez's mother Pilar (Mildred Dunnock), who still lives in San Martín, offers Viñolas a unique opportunity to catch his man. Viñolas has her brought to the town hospital where he can entrap Artiguez. She dies there, but Viñolas sends Carlos (Raymond Pellegrin), a turncoat trusted by Artiguez, to lure him by concealing the fact and preying on his sense of honor. At the same time, he is sought out by Paco (Carlo Angeletti), the ten-year-old son of a former comrade tortured to death by Viñolas whom Paco wants Artiguez to avenge. Artiguez refuses him, throwing the boy out with the angry exclamation that he has fought enough.

At this point, an unlikely intercessor appears in the person of the priest Francisco (Omar Sharif), who has attended Pilar on her deathbed. Despite her knowledge that the Church colludes with Viñolas' plot, Pilar, seeing personal decency in Francisco, entrusts him with a note warning Manuel against attempting to visit her. Torn between clerical discipline and his sense of obligation to a deathbed wish, Francisco agrees to deliver it on his way to a pilgrimage at Lourdes. Not finding Artiguez and unaware of Paco's identity, he leaves the note with the child. Paco destroys it, but confesses his act when Pedro reveals his own suspicions of Carlos. Determined to get at the truth, Artiguez kidnaps Francisco at Lourdes, but Carlos, his plot discovered, overpowers him and flees. Humiliated by this, Artiguez keeps Francisco captive, partly as an assertion of power and partly from an unacknowledged need for consolation. Discovering that Francisco hails from a neighboring village, Artiguez turns his captive into company, and finally releases him.

Knowing that Pilar has died, Artiguez nonetheless determines to fulfill his mission, even if it is only to pay respects to a corpse that, in all likelihood, he will join with his own. Two brief scenes give us insight into what has become for him, finally, a purely personal journey. As he takes to the road he sees Pedro, already drunk, outside the café whose young waitress tidies it for the morning trade. Paying Pedro's bill, his gaze falls on the girl's exposed leg, and, feeling its penetration, she rises before him. We understand Artiguez's manhood revived in this moment, and the battle he is nerved to fight.

Artiguez tells Pedro that he is going to San Martín alone. When Pedro asks what purpose this will serve with Pilar dead, he shrugs in reply, "What else can I do?" Needing no more, Pedro grunts his assent. Without words, honor is understood.

The story proceeds to its inevitable conclusion. Artiguez crosses Pyrenees paths well-worn in memory, the camera following him at one point as he crosses an arched passage as if entering his fate: an image perhaps a beat too long in a film that does not otherwise waste a frame. He flags down a car whose terrified driver take him to San Martín and reports his presence at once. Viñolas' men, alerted, take up their posts.

What, at this point, remains of Artiguez's errand? He will not see his mother, well-guarded in the morgue. He wants to kill the traitor Carlos, and presumably Viñolas, in the final act of their long duel. With that, his war will at last be over. He picks off Carlos and wounds Viñolas, who comes up lame, perhaps marked for good by his adversary. He takes a few of the *Guardia* with him, and dies in a hail of bullets. He is laid out side by side with Pilar, proof as they lie together that, mother and son, the ghost of the Civil War is being laid to rest as well.

The penultimate scene of the film shows a limping but exuberant Viñolas, accompanied by his men, taking a victory lap. Asked for his reaction to the death of his great antagonist, Viñolas says that he has merely eliminated a "bandit." The question that will persist, however, grafted into the very wound Artiguez has given him, is why the cunningest of men, knowing the trap set for him, would walk deliberately into it. For one man, at least, the ghost of the war will not rest: Viñolas himself.

The film's last scene contains no dialogue: it is the scene again of *High Noon*, as the townspeople of San Martín gather silently in the square behind Viñolas, uncertain of what has truly taken place. Indeed, its meaning will belong neither to Artiguez nor Viñolas but to those who must ultimately find their future defined by it.

The film's own story is reflected in its subject matter. Its preview audiences showed puzzlement over its context, memories having faded of what had once been the conflict of a generation, and Zinnemann was obliged to insert footage from a contemporary documentary, *To Die in Madrid,* as a headnote to his own film. If, however, audiences and critics responded coolly to it, one constituency did not. The Franco regime, still in power, roundly condemned it and did its best to suppress its distribution. Despite the support of its producer, Columbia Pictures, it lost money and would soon fade from view. Zinnemann next directed *A Man for All Seasons,* likewise a film about a single man defying a tyrannical regime, which won him Academy awards for best director and best picture. *Behold a Pale Horse* remains to this day his most underrated and in some ways his most important film.

To grasp the film's full intentions, we must consider it as a further reflection on the themes of *High Noon.* In *High Noon,* a lawman seeks to protect a frontier town from the disorder into which it may relapse if the villain who threatens it is not confronted. Will Kane may be a complex and partly conflicted figure, but Frank Miller is not. His approach promises violence and anarchy. Manuel Artiguez, too, menaces the order of San Martín; he too conducts 'banditry' and threatens the established order. His purposes, however, are diametrically opposed to Miller's. The order that reigns in San Martín is that of fascism, instituted by violence, sustained by oppression, and cemented by an unholy alliance of church and state. Artiguez fights it with the tools at his disposal. His cause may be lost but it is not unjust, nor is it to be abandoned. It is not, as Miller's is, to extinguish conscience but to rekindle it. The aging guerilla's manners may be coarsened; his means may be peccant; his destiny is tragic. His intent is not, however, to extinguish conscience and hope, but to rekindle them. If he can do no more, he fights to the end to keep memory alive.

The townspeople who assemble around Will Kane at the end of *High Noon* array themselves around the only remaining authority in the community. At the moment when Kane drops his badge in the dust, that community is suspended if not dissolved. Miller and his gang are dead, but Kane's gesture is a comment on a town that, morally, no longer exists. The new marshal will arrive to whatever falsehoods may await him; his tenure, however we may imagine it, will not be a happy one. Courage alone cannot make a community, nor, if unvalued or unshared, preserve it.

The crowd that gathers in San Martín is thus not one of community but the absence of one. Something has happened; there has been a battle, and some are dead. There will be an official explanation, which will be accepted as far as needs be. The inhabitants of the town will go back to their accustomed lives; there are no citizens here. Manuel Artiguez has given his life, partly for reasons of personal honor and partly to bequeath his native town a riddle to be solved. The autocracy of Francisco Franco would last another decade and a half, Franco himself fading into a long twilight and his regime, the remnant of another era, collapsing with his death. Spain itself, as Pedro Almodóvar's recent film *Parallel Mothers* has made clear, is still literally exhuming its dead.

Gary Cooper's Major Thorn represents another aspect of the dialogue between courage and community. Thorn's attempt to create a community *of* courage is fatally misconstrued, because physical courage alone, however requisite in battle, is not readily translatable to civic virtue. Thorn's heroes are mostly opportunists if not desperadoes, and their medals meaningless to them as such. It is the slow unfolding of his own moral courage—the principled determination to protect the weak and injured in his charge—that far more reflects the community he seeks, even if it is he who has put them in peril. In the end, as the awards book reveals, what he finally attempts to understand is not the courage that only crisis can summon in a few but the humanity that must be sought for in all. When Chawk reads out its final pages, he understands no more of them than Thorn has done in attempting to isolate courage from its occasion, but only that he has found something perhaps rarer: charity. It will not, in all likelihood, make for more than the moment's cohesion as the men descend to Cordura; but it is a moment.

Courage is, of course, a perennial theme, especially in film, and community is often entwined with it. The shock of World War II and its aftermath brought both issues into higher relief, and not in American cinema alone; one thinks, for example, of Roberto Rossellini's *Open City* and Carol Reed's *Odd Man Out*. Zinnemann, like his European confreres seeking refuge in America, would give it a more grimly etched vision of itself in the idiom of film noir. The hospitality would be returned during the McCarthy persecution, when blacklisted American actors, directors, and screenwriters found their own moral courage tested, as Robert Rossen's was: nor should we regard it as merely accidental that the protagonist of his *They Came to Cordura* would be a self-indicted coward seeking redemption.

The conventional view of postwar American cinema as largely reflecting a culture of consumerism and global dominion is thus a far from adequate account of its complexities and anxieties, and the questions posed by its more searching observers. Home and community, so those engaged in history's greatest war were told, were the values for which it was fought; courage and sacrifice were the means by which it was won. But truth comes mostly in shades of gray, and often those shades are the darkest.

Endnotes

1. "The Bloody Sire," in Tim Hunt, ed., *The Collected Poetry of Robinson Jeffers, 5 vols.* (Stanford UP, 1988-2001), 3: 25.

2. In an otherwise taut plot this is the one gaping hole, for if Kane is to take the noon train on which Miller arrives, he will immediately be confronted by them.

3. Its screenwriter, Carl Foreman, was subsequently blacklisted. He eventually made a second career as a respected figure in British film.

4. Rossen had previously won acclaim as the director of *All the King's Men* and would subsequently direct *The Hustler* before his premature death.

5. The film's title, which cites one of the Bible's most dramatic images, references the enduring legacy of the Spanish Civil War, but more subtly one of its early episodes in which Viñolas, admiring a horse he has ridden, compels its owner into a reluctant sale. The moment appears forgotten until the film's end when Viñolas reflects that he must return the horse in an atonement that, only half understood, suggests the possibility of a moral awakening. It is also with the release of the horses to Arreaga's men in *They Came to Cordura* too that the crisis of that film is precipitated.

Dan Farkas

HEMINGWAY AND THE BOWLING BALL

Ernest Hemingway advised, "…write one true sentence, write the truest sentence that you know."

It happened in Chicago. That much is true. The ending? Also, true. The trappings? They are true enough. Forty years of time have trivialized the minor details.

They had been college roommates in East Lansing. Now, one was in law school, the other preparing for a career in biotech. The weekend was to be one of revelry. They were too young to realize they were creating lifelong memories to warm old men's hearts in the next century. This was a weekend meant for devouring college basketball, Chicago deep-dish pizza, and blues at The Checkerboard Lounge. There would be lying and boasting about girlfriends, and pot… lots and lots of pot.

It was a Friday and while there was no basketball or blues to be had at 11 AM on a pristine, frigid, February morning, there was marijuana and camaraderie. Breakfast was bagels piled high with cream cheese, lox, tomatoes, and red onion slivers. The greasy spoon's waitress reported there were no capers and brought tall refills of cold chocolate milk by way of apology. They chose the Museum of Science and Industry as the day's entertainment.

They debated transportation: Chicago's El vs. the '73 baby blue Chevy Caprice. They decided the Blue Bomb afforded greater opportunity for indulging; warm and out of sight of nosy looks. Al Green's soulful voice played through the Chevy's tinny speakers while they lingered over a fat joint, passed back and forth until only a tiny nub that had no herb left to burn was flicked out the window.

The Hawk bit hard as they exited the car. They snugged up their puffy down coats, pulled their stocking caps down lower. They were buffeted about by the wind, shivering, as they traversed the few hundred yards from the distant parking lot to the Museum's entrance. Inside, the Museum was vast and held a chill.

To describe the museum would dilute Hemingway's advice on truth. Did they pass a display on nuclear energy? Had there been a submarine or biplane suspended from the ceiling? Was there a gift shop? Yes. No. Maybe. It doesn't matter. It was a museum. It was grand, marbled, full of things, and smelled of lime-based disinfectant. The marijuana undermined hope of memory for unimportant details; four decades have erased minutiae altogether. The drug's influence played the starring role in amplifying the singular event that stands erect among graying neurons; the tale of the bowling ball.

They climbed a grand, circular staircase with an outsized landing that opened to an exhibit hall. At the entrance to the hall was a display, seven feet high, twice as long, perhaps a yard wide. On a squat, wooden base, the color of a well-used baseball bat, were four plexiglass walls. Another sheet of plexiglass topped the case.

Along the bottom of the big glass box was a metallic track big enough to accommodate a bowling ball. Just such a faded ball nested at one end of the track. There was scaffolding that served as an elevator chute for the ball's eventual ascent toward the top of the case. At the apex, the ball's cradle would engage with a canted upper track that would guide the ball downward to the opposite end of the case where it would land with a thud in the bottom track, angled so the ball could return to its cradle and begin the process anew.

There were no signs. There was no placard providing education about gravity or conversion of potential energy to kinetic energy. There was only the big glass box, its imprisoned bowling ball, and a smooth oak handle attached to a crank that protruded from the side of the case where the ball rested, waiting to engage in its next cycle. The invitation was obvious. Turn the crank. See something happen.

A young mother indulged her small child in the exercise. The boy labored, gravity pulling hard on the 16 pound ball. Each 360 degree turn of the handle was rewarded with only a few new inches of height. Mom, resigned, rolled her eyes. The child worked with tenacity, leaning in on tipped toes.

The marijuana-influenced pair of friends settled in to watch, mesmerized. They shared their prevailing thought without words, using several smirk-tinged, side-long glances at each other during the ball's slow-motion elevator ride. This kid was working his ass off. He was invested. What was all this effort going to come to? Would it be worth it? Was the juice worth the squeeze?

Two minutes in; a long time to wait and watch. The kid was breathing hard. The ball was near the top. The drama's climax was imminent. A few museum patrons had gathered to see the action.

And finally...the denouement. The ball reached the top of the scaffolding and its cradle clicked, engaging with the track. It rolled downward at a shallow angle, reached the side of the case furthest from the crank—BOOM—nestled into the track that ran along the bottom, and rolled slowly back to its original resting place. Thunk!

The "action," brief, obvious, and predictable, had taken mere seconds. The ball rolled down, the ball returned to rest. It was an "event" completely disproportionate to the amount of time and effort the child had expended.

The laugh that ignited in the friends' drugged brains exploded from both of them a pregnant instant after the old roommates exchanged a look of amazement. They became consumed, doubled over, struggling to find breath. By the time they had gathered themselves, the child and his mother, the few spectators; all had dispersed. They were alone, left to wipe tears from their eyes and wonder.

Was the whole episode a commentary on the futility of life? Put in a ton of effort and then be rewarded with what? Nothing much. Was that too cynical a view for men still in their salad days? Was it the pot? Was it pitying cockiness? Was it self-deprecating, realizing they had just wasted time for no good reason?

In reflection, it was all of those things though, in the moment, it was largely the pot. At bottom, the philosophy of it doesn't matter. What matters is the memory of a joint laugh, a marker of shared experience, an emotion so true that it burns brightly 40 years later and honors well Hemingway's direction to write the truth:

There is joy in remembering joy.

Joseph H. Tyson

MATT TALBOT: "VENERABLE" FOREVER?

Substance abuse has become a major problem in today's world. 21 million Americans have at least one addiction, but less than 10% get treatment. Addicts in the 21ˢᵗ Century not only consume alcohol, tobacco, and marijuana, but heroin, cocaine, methamphetamine, Fentanyl, Ecstasy, etc. 107,000 Americans died from drug overdoses in 2021—up from 93,000 in 2020, and 72,000 in 2019. Most O.D. victims are under forty.

Though de-criminalization sounds great to libertarians, studies have proven that usage and addiction increase after legalization. Alcohol consumption fell 30% in 1919 after enactment of the 18ᵗʰ Amendment which prohibited the manufacture and sale of intoxicating liquors. By 1933, the year of Prohibition's repeal, alcoholic beverage sales climbed 65% higher than the 1918 total.

For centuries St. Matthias the Apostle has been the Catholic Church's patron saint of alcoholics. We know next to nothing about him. According to legend he became a disciple of Jesus after being baptized by John the Baptist. Following Jesus's death, and Judas's suicide, the remaining eleven apostles cast lots to elect Matthias as the twelfth apostle. He allegedly preached Christ's message in Ethiopia. How he came to be the patron of inebriates has been lost in the mists of time. Was he a reformed drunk himself? No one has a clue.

With no disrespect intended toward St. Matthias, Catholics in Ireland have proposed Venerable Matt Talbot as the modern patron of alcoholics, drug addicts, and their families.

The second of twelve children, Matthew Talbot was born on May 2, 1856 into the family of Dublin dock worker Charles Talbot and Elizabeth Bagnall Talbot. In 1868, after a few years of sporadic education, twelve year old Matt got his first job as a messenger boy for wine merchants Edward and John Burke, who also bottled Guinness Stout. Imitating the example of other employees, Matt helped himself to pints of Guinness while at work, and became an alcoholic by age thirteen. In 1872 he moved on to a higher paying job in the Port & Docks' stores, which daily handled innumerable cases of hard liquor. Consequently, Matt began drinking whiskey. Young Talbot's tippling seemed quite natural since father Charles, and most of his uncles, brothers, and friends drank heavily.

Matt's friend Pat Doyle said of the male Talbots:

> "All of (them), father and sons, drank; all barring John, the eldest....
> Old Charlie and the boys were always arguing. ... On Saturdays when
> they'd all had a good drop in, they were a contrary lot..."

Pat asserted that Matt drank compulsively between 1868 and 1884, without
regard for others. "He wouldn't go with us to a dance, party, or school function. He only wanted to drink."

In 1873 Pemberton Construction Co. hired seventeen year old Matt as a
laborer. Though an energetic worker, who foremen regularly selected to set
the pace for other hod-carriers, he blew most of his wages on booze, and
sometimes missed work due to hangovers. On September 21, 1874 police
arrested 18 year old Matt for assault. A magistrate sentenced him to a month
in jail.

When low on funds, Talbot would pawn his watch, boots, coat, and other
possessions for money to squander in pubs. He once robbed and pawned a
street musician's fiddle in order to get drunk.

One day in early 1884, when broke between paychecks, 28 year old Matt
asked several mates at O'Meara's Pub to buy him a drink. None obliged.
Disgusted, Talbot trudged home and told his mother he intended to take
the pledge. She advised him not to do so unless he meant to abide by it. The
next Saturday he went to Holy Cross College in Clonliffe, one of Dublin's
seminaries for educating priests, and swore to abstain from alcohol for three
months. He subsequently renewed his vow for another three months, then a
year. His first two years of temperance were particularly hard. To avoid the
urge to drink after work, he would eat an early dinner, then pray in various
churches until sacristans informed him it was time to lock up for the night.
On May 14, 1890 Matt signed The Total Abstinence League of the Sacred
Heart's Heroic Offering for Life.

Once sober, Talbot grew pious and responsible. He began attending daily
Mass, confessed his sins once a week, and paid his debts to publicans. Fail-
ing to find the fiddler whose violin he'd stolen, Matt donated money to the
Dominican fathers to have Masses said for his prosperity and salvation.

Talbot joined such organizations as Sodality of the Blessed Virgin Mary, St.
Vincent DePaul Society, Perpetual Lamp Association, Arch-Confraternity

of Bona Mors (Happy Death), and Pioneer Total Abstinence Association. On October 18, 1891 he was consecrated as a lay Franciscan brother. In his role as an Oblate of St. Francis Matt helped the poor and sick. He generously contributed to Catholic charities, including Father John C. Drumgoole's New York City Orphanage Association, The Crusade for Preservation of Holy Shrines, the Poor Clares' Convent in Keady, and the Columban priests' missions to China.

In the words of Talbot's former Vice Procurator, Father Morgan Costolloe, "When Matt found sobriety through prayer and spiritual guidance, his (craving) for drink was replaced by a desire for Christian perfection." Talbot-advocate Father Brian Lawless pointed out that "Matt's spiritual approach prefigured the 12-Step (program) to recovery formulated by A.A."

Friends described Matt in his mid-thirties as short, wiry, and slope-shouldered, with gray-streaked brown hair. Though sometimes shabbily-dressed, he was always neat and clean.-Among his personality traits were candor, determination, kindness, generosity, courage, and industriousness. Since childhood he had a tendency to walk fast with his eyes cast down.

Circa 1892 Talbot obtained a position with Messers T. & C. Martin, Ltd., a firm located on the Liffey River's bank which sold lumber, furniture, cement, fertilizers, and other supplies. At first he had to do heavy work: loading and unloading timber into trucks, stacking wood, and shoving planks in and out of vats filled with hot creosote. Although Matt seldom complained, he did mention to his foreman that it bothered him to have his work clothes smelling faintly of tar and guano when he received communion each morning at 6:30 Mass.

Due to his demonstrated integrity, Matt soon became "storekeeper," or inventory clerk, in one of T. & C. Martin's warehouses. Supervisor Edward Carew also entrusted him with the company's keys, and responsibility for opening the yard's front gate every workday at 8 A. M. sharp. His new post required him to make mathematical calculations. In Catholic school Matt learned how to read, write, add, subtract, and pray, but he apparently played hooky when multiplication and division were taught. To make up for that gap in his knowledge, he kept a "Ready Reckoner" card in his pocket, which provided multiplication tables for numbers 2 through 12.

Matt read Catholic literature on social justice, as well as Pope Leo XIII's 1891 Encyclical, Rerum Novarum. From those essays he gleaned the truth that no one has the right to starve the poor into submission. Believing that blue collar laborers deserved a living wage, Matt joined the Irish Transport & General Workers Union on September 22, 1911, and faithfully paid dues until becoming disabled in June, 1923. Although he neither attended union meetings nor picketed any businesses, Matt did not oppose the Dublin Lockout Strike which occurred between August 26, 1913 and January 18, 1914. Talbot initially refused to accept strike pay from the union because he hadn't earned it. He later decided to take the money in order to distribute it to fellow workmen with families.

Martin's employees related anecdotes about Matt. During lunch breaks, and intervals between shipping, receiving, and storing, he generally went to an area in the drying shed to pray alone. Talbot preferred not to mingle with the dockworkers who unloaded timber from ships because of their incessant cursing. When men around him used foul language, he would whip out a crucifix from his pocket, hold it aloft, and declare: "Look, boys, see who you are insulting!" Matt refused to listen to off-color jokes. A co-worker quoted him as saying: "You cannot avoid hearing, but you need not laugh at a dirty story." One day an argument ensued when a warehouseman's wife dropped off lunch to him. The employee used obscene language as he railed at her. After Matt walked over to him and said, "Jesus Christ is listening to you," the man hung his head in shame.

One day a workmate who'd arrived late dashed into the warehouse and hid behind a stack of lumber. An instant later one of the company's directors burst in and asked Matt if he'd seen that individual. Matt replied: "I wish you would not ask me these questions, sir; you know I do not wish to answer them." After the boss angrily strode out of the building, Matt said to the tardy man: "Did you hear that? Attend to it! I will not tell lies to save you."

Matt always gave generously whenever men at Martin's took up collections for employees who'd suffered illnesses, injuries, or other misfortunes. However, he always told them to come back the next day. Matt rarely carried cash with him to avoid the temptation of dropping into one of his old haunts to drink.

Following his father's death in 1899 Matt lived with his mother Elizabeth at 18 Upper Rutland St. in Dublin. After she died in 1915, Matt moved to an apartment on Gloucester St. He paid his sister, Mrs. Mary Andrews, to cook and clean. She attested that he fasted often, abstained from meat four days per week, as well as all during Advent and Lent. For breakfast he ate only a dry piece of bread with tea or cocoa. .

To deepen his understanding of Catholic theology, Matt improved his reading skills and enrolled in classes at Holy Cross College in Clonliffe. One of his teachers remarked that it was a shame that such a studious individual had not gone further in school, to which he replied: "God knew best." Matt principally studied the Bible, religious publications, and Catholic classics such as *The Confessions of St. Augustine*, St. Francis DeSales' *Introduction to a Devout Life*, *Spiritual Exercises* by St. Ignatius Loyola, Cardinal John Newman's *Apologia Pro Vita*, and St. Louis Marie de Montfort's *True Devotion to the Blessed Virgin*. He especially admired saints who had been reformed sinners. The conversions of Mary Magdalene, Augustine of Hippo, Mary of Egypt, and Ignatius Loyola displayed God's might. Matt believed that he'd experienced the same divine power in his own life.

Matt chose Monsignor Michael Hickey, a philosophy professor at Holy Cross College, as his spiritual counselor. Monsignor Hickey introduced him to the 6th Century Irish Monastic Rule. This early version of Irish Christianity taught that humans had a concupiscent nature which could only be subdued through prayer, fasting, the sacraments, scripture reading, wholesome work, and good deeds. Medieval Irish monks transmuted pagan Celtic polytheism into veneration for the Trinity, Blessed Virgin Mary, angels, and saints.

Matt's devotions gradually became more strenuous. During Lent he followed The Stations of the Cross at St. Francis Xavier's Church on his knees. Matt typically attended several masses on Sundays—not only at St. Francis Xavier, but St. Theresa's Church on Clarendon St., St. Laurence O'Toole's Church, the Franciscans' "Adam & Eve" Church, St. Joseph's Church on Berkley Road, St. Savior's Dominican Church, and the Pro-Cathedral. On Sunday, August 22, 1915 Matt wrote in his journal: "On Feast of Seven Joys, Blessed Virgin Mary, August 22nd, 1915, I was present at twenty-one Masses," which must be a world record.

Future President of Ireland Sean T. O'Kelly served as an altar boy at St. Francis Xavier Church in the early 1890's. He and his mates liked friendly Matt, who greeted them by their first names. Sean stated that some of the boys dubbed him "Holy Joe" because of his extreme piety. He personally thought Matt's godliness extraordinary rather than excessive, and later visited his tomb in Glasnevin Cemetery.

Matt never performed tasks half-heartedly. His friend Pat Doyle once said of him: "He could never go easy at anything." To mortify the flesh Matt practiced austerities. He slept on a wooden plank; a block of wood served as his pillow, and burlap sack as a blanket. (That hard "pillow" caused facial numbness, and eventually impaired his hearing.)

Matt's weekday routine consisted of rising at 4:30 AM, attending Mass, then having tea and unbuttered bread for breakfast. After working all day, he returned to his lonely apartment for a light supper, put on his suit, and set off for religious activities. Those included Sodality meetings and evening services such as benediction, novenas, Adoration of the Blessed Sacrament, and Stations of the Cross. Upon returning home Matt would read the Bible, say a rosary, and sing hymns before retiring around 10:30 PM. Into his plank bed he brought a statue of Mary holding infant Jesus.

Sixty-eight year old Matt had to be hospitalized in Mater Misericordia Hospital for heart and kidney ailments from June 19th to July 17th, 1923, then again between September 10th and October 27th of that same year. Physicians diagnosed him with tachycardia (fast beating heart) and nephritis. While bedridden Matt prayed, said the rosary, and read his Bible. When his strength returned, he spent hours praying in the hospital's chapel.

Right before Matt's discharge on October 27th, 1923, cardiologist Dr. Moore, warned him that tachycardia patients usually die suddenly. His sisters Mary and Susan urged him to carry identification with him. Matt shrugged and said the matter was in God's hands. When they recommended another heart specialist, and the possibility of taking digitalis to control his heart arrhythmia, he replied: "Nobody can keep me if Our Lord wants me."

In spite of poor health, Matt insisted upon returning to work, so he could continue sending charitable donations. T & C. Martin's welcomed him back in April, 1925.

On Trinity Sunday, June 7, 1925 sixty-nine year old Matt collapsed while walking down Granby Lane, headed for 10 o' clock Mass. Shopkeeper Mrs. Anne Keogh tried to assist, but he died as she tried to give him a drink of water. The instant he breathed his last, church bells rang, heralding the start of Mass. Father Reginald Walsh administered the last rites as Matt lay supine on the pavement. None of those on the scene remembered his name. Police officer O'Hanlon summoned an ambulance which transported Matt's lifeless body to Jervis Hospital, where Dr. Hannigan pronounced him dead.

Susan Talbot Fylan banged on the door of his neighbor Francis Donnellan later that day and exclaimed: "Matt's missing!" Mr. Donnellan accompanied her to Fitzgibbon St. police station where she made a report. The police contacted Mrs. Fylan the next morning, and asked her to meet them at Jervis Hospital's mortuary. There she tearfully identified Matt. Medical examiners conducted a brief inquest before releasing his body. The coroner listed myocardial degeneration as cause of death.

Hospital orderlies Charles Manners and Laurence Thornton found chains, cords, and beads wrapped around Matt's corpse. Nursing supervisor Sister Mary Ignatius told them to send those items to the undertaker along with his body.

Family members, neighbors, co-workers, priests, and nuns attended Matt's Requiem Mass at St. Savior Church. He was buried in Glasnevin Cemetery wearing the brown habit of a third order Franciscan. Matt's chains, ropes, medals, a scapular, rosary beads, and other sacramental objects were placed in his coffin. His body was exhumed in 1952 and moved to Glasnevin's vault. Ten years later the Archdiocese of Dublin transferred his remains to a tomb inside Our Lady of Lourdes Church.

Dubliners of every stripe visited Talbot's grave in Glasnevin Cemetery, bringing flowers, holy cards, statuettes, written messages, etc. The Catholic Church takes seriously vox populi, which means public recognition of a holy person.

Wine merchant Raphael "Ralph" O'Callaghan had been acquainted with Matt since 1912 from Sodality at St. Francis Xavier Church. He endorsed him as a candidate for sainthood to Dublin Archbishop Edward J. Byrne, who authorized an inquiry on November 16, 1931. Over the next two decades at least three popular books promoted Matt's canonization: barrister Sir Joseph A. Glynn's *Life of Matt Talbot* (1928); *We Knew Matt Talbot* (1948) by Rev. Albert H. Dolan; and Mary Purcell's *Matt Talbot and His Times* (1954).

After amassing a file on Matt, Archbishop Byrne's staff referred his case to the Vatican. In 1937 Rome agreed to consider the Archdiocese's petition. Following an investigation by the Curia's Congregation for the Causes of Saints, Pope Pius XII gave Matt Talbot the title Servant of God on May 3rd, 1947. After more research by the Congregation, Pope Paul VI declared him "Venerable" on October 3, 1975.

The Roman Catholic Church's Curia, a conclave of cardinals and bishops, oversees the Informative Process which vets potential saints. It employs dozens of ecclesiastical officials. Scholarly "relators" gather data about candidates' genealogies, life histories, letters, journals, and published writings (if any). A "postulator" appointed by the Curia acts as a judge. "Procurators" champion the holy person's cause. "Devil's advocates" attempt to find fault with nominees. After proceedings end, the postulator forwards a "posito," or "trial transcript," along with supporting documents, to a panel of nine theologians which votes for or against beatification. Those experts submit their recommendations to the Curia and pope for a decision.

Although the Church conducts such inquiries under a cloak of secrecy, it does not forbid procurators from publicly praising their candidates. Matt Talbot's current Vice Procurator, Father Brian Lawless, hailed him as a heroically virtuous member of the laboring class.

> "Matt was a poor working man from Dublin.... Part of his charm and endearment is that he's just like us—one of the little guys."

Father Lawless lamented that not enough "first class" miracles had materialized to qualify Matt for beatification. To the media he stated:

> "In order for his cause to go through, there has to be a verifiable event. There might be miracles all over the place thanks to his intercession, but they aren't reported. No one knows about them."

However, Sir Joseph A. Glynn had enumerated miracles ascribed to Matt in the 5th (1934) edition of his book. A few seemed to meet the "first class" standard. For example, after surgery which removed her adenoids and tonsils, a thirteen year old girl became critically ill. Following subsequent operations for mastoid and a middle ear infection, general septicemia set in. A specialist pronounced her condition "absolutely hopeless." Shortly after her parents applied one of Talbot's relics to the girl's body, her downward spiral ceased, and she made a full recovery.

In 1933 a German Jesuit priest from Walkenburg testified:

> "A boy, six years old, was confined to bed ... entirely unconscious ... for days with a dangerous skull fracture. The physician gave no hope. At noon I handed a fragment of Matt Talbot's wooden pillow to the (nursing) sister who attached it to the boy's shirt. When his mother

approached him (soon thereafter), he opened his eyes (and asked for something to drink.)"

Matt Talbot's long-delayed canonization mystifies me. Mother Teresa and Pope John Paul II became saints within nine years of their deaths, and deservedly so. But why has the process for Matt Talbot taken so long? The stalled deliberations for his cause have dragged on for 91 years—through the reigns of eight popes, plus multiple procurators, relators, postulators, prefects, and devil's advocates. What's the hold-up? Because of those proceedings' clandestine nature, we can only guess.

One stumbling block appears to be Matt's "austerities," which played less well in mid-20th century Rome than early 1930's Ireland. Penitential disciplines involving chains, cords, iron beds without mattresses, hair shirts, etc. went out of fashion soon after Austrian Dr. Richard Krafft-Ebbing wrote *Psychopathia Sexualis* in 1886. What Krafft-Ebbing termed "masochism" (after decadent nobleman Leopold von Ritter Sacher-Masoch) violated the Commandment, "Thou shalt not kill," which forbids not only murder, but harm done to oneself and others. In 1977 Matt's procurator enlisted priest-psychiatrist Dr. Eamon Feichin O'Doherty to testify at a closed Curia hearing. He explained that masochists endure various forms of physical and psychological maltreatment in order to achieve perverse sexual gratification. In Dr. O'Doherty's professional opinion, Matt practiced asceticism solely for spiritual purposes.

Nevertheless, journalist Emmett Oliver sparked a furor in December, 1996 by condemning what he called Talbot's "extreme self-abuse." Others associated Matt's program of self-mortification with Jansenism, a 17th Century heresy set forth by Dutch bishop Cornelius Jansen which emphasized Original Sin, humankind's depravity, and the necessity for self-abnegation. Church theologians proscribed Jansenism because it implied that omniscient and benevolent God had either botched Creation, or intentionally created a species of diabolical malefactors (namely us).

By the 1980's Matt's proponents stressed his piety, devotion to the Church, and philanthropic acts, while downplaying his harsh regime of self-discipline.

Matt was a dedicated servant of Mary, Mother of Jesus. That might have adversely affected his cause for sainthood during the Feeney Scandal. In 1940 Catherine Goddard Clarke founded The Slaves of the Immaculate

Heart of Mary at St. Benedict Center near Harvard College in Cambridge, Massachusetts. Jesuit priest Leonard Feeney became the Slaves' chaplain in 1945. Under his leadership, the organization grew increasingly radical. Jesuit superiors reprimanded Feeney for espousing "Maryolatry," a movement which worshipped the Blessed Mother as a goddess. They also chastised him for promoting the false doctrine that only Catholics could enter Heaven. Just when the Holocaust's horrors were being publicized, Feeney decried Jews as "perpetual enemies of Christ." (It apparently slipped his mind that Jesus and Mary were Jewish.) When he refused to obey a directive from Jesuit superiors which transferred him from St. Benedict Center to Holy Cross College, they expelled Feeney from the order. Boston Archbishop Richard J. Cushing ruled The Slaves of Mary a heretical sect, and forbade Catholics to have any connection with it. In 1953 Pope Pius XII excommunicated Leonard Feeney from the Church for heresy.

Although Matt Talbot venerated Jesus's mother, he never advocated her deification, nor subscribed to the notion that God denied salvation to Protestants, Jews, Buddhists, Muslims, etc. In the Feeney flap's aftermath, would too ardent devotion to Mary count against a person nominated for beatification?

"The grainy photograph here [L] is the only known image of [Matt Talbot], enlarged from a group photo taken at his one-time place of employ." [R]

Sources: www.improbable.com; www.abbey-roads.blogspot.com

Many find Talbot's example very relevant. In 2014 Father Richard Ebejer told reporters:

> "We want to present Matt Talbot as a model for young people. (Some) think of him as an old man, but his conversion was at 28. He can speak to today's young people."

Over 50,000 recovering alcoholics and drug addicts now belong to the Matt Talbot Retreat Movement. That organization has opened rehabilitation facilities in Ireland, England, Poland, the U.S., Australia, and elsewhere. Matt's religious solution offers hope to the afflicted. As Father Brian Lawless put it:

> "Matt is highly regarded in the U. S. With all the difficulties people are facing, now's the time (they) need a patron… He's the obvious choice."

The altar boys who called Matt Talbot "Holy Joe" perceived him as fanatical. Has Matt's rigorous sanctity hurt his chances for sainthood?

Endnotes

1. Mary Purcell, *Matt Talbot and his Times*, Franciscan Herald Press, Chicago, 1977 (reprint of 1954 edition), p. 24.

2. Ibid., p. 134.

3. Sir Joseph A. Glynn, *The Life of Matt Talbot*, Catholic Truth Society of Ireland, Dublin, 1934, pp. 14-15.

4. Ibid., p. 15.

5. Ibid., pp. 15-16.

6. Father Morgan Costolloe, "Matt Talbot's Canonization Would be a Sign of Hope to Alcoholics," *The Irish Times*, January 14, 1997.

7. Gina Christian, "From Sot to Saint: Matt Talbot Gives Hope for Recovery from Addiction," *Arlington Catholic Herald*, September 17, 2018.

8. Purcell, p. 97.

9. Ibid., p. 92.

10. Ibid., p. 186.

11. Ibid., p. 178.

12. Glynn, p. 24.

13. Ibid., pp. 23-24.

14. Purcell, p. 181.

15. Ibid.

16. Ibid., p. 153.

17. Purcell, p. 103.

18. Glynn, p. 83.

19. Purcell, p. 107.

20. Ibid.

21. Glynn, p. 65.

22. Purcell, p. 220.

23. Ibid., p. 68.

24. Ibid., p. 119.

25. Ibid., pp. 91-92.

26. Ibid., p. 91.

27. Ibid., 297.

28. Ibid., p. 214.

29. Glynn, p. 99.

30. Purcell, p. 225.

31. Ibid., p. 229.

32. Jane Walsh, "On This Day (June 7th): Matt Talbot, Potentially Ireland's Next Saint, Died in 1924," *Irish Central*, June 7, 2021.

33. Joe Bollig, "The Making of a Miracle," *The Leaven*, September 26, 2014.

34. Glynn, p. 102.

35. Ibid., pp. 102-103.

36. Ibid., pp. 104-105 .

37. Mags Gargan, "New Miracle May Put Matt Talbot on the Road to Sainthood," *The Irish Catholic*, January 1, 2015.

Ray Greenblatt

PETERSBURG BY ANDREI BELY

A Book Review

James Joyce's *Ulysses* (1918) observed the middle class of Dublin. The first installment of Marcel Proust's *In Search of Lost Time* (1913) delved into the upper class of Paris. Andrei Bely's novel *Petersburg*, a panorama of all classes in Russia, also came out in 1913 in entirety but was not translated into English until 1959.

STYLISTICS

Bely is as uniquely experimental as Joyce or Proust. Petersburg is a voluminous book, nearly 600 pages, as many Russian novels are. I use the word "stylistics" to underscore his one-of-a-kind, often poetic writing. The book consists of eight chapters running from fifty to one hundred pages each. Many untitled sections of various length make up each chapter. Poems are often included. One very singular technique is to indent an entire paragraph mostly focused on emotional moments in characters' lives.

From time to time Bely pops into the scene to comment. "Let the reader forgive me: I shall express the essence of this gaze in a most banal word: love." He uses direct address dramatically. "Only in you has the memory of Petrine Petersburg remained."

He repeats words, phrases, even entire sentences for emphasis and to maintain a rhythm. "In this place and that place and that place there was a strike, that in this place and that place and that place a strike was in preparation, that people were going to strike—in this place, in this place and this place."

He employs series of verbs. "Suddenly her eyes stopped, dilated, blinked, crossed."A series of adverbs: "Angrily, vividly, distinctly, Sergei . . . ." Often a triad of participles: "Varvara . . . was somewhere over there, flailing, struggling, pushing." These adjectival forms could be compound: "a cat-smelling, half-torn, worn-through carpet."

The author uses sharpened sense imagery. Smell is depicted. "A smell of warmed-up dirt that had been brought in from the street on boots." Or even an echo of Kafka. "A revulsion, as at an enormous insect whose shell gives off a savour of nauseating tin; there was something part-insect, part-unplated metal dish about it."

But he is a master of sounds. "The autumnal season's old woman's whisper came to his ears." "The gramophone's tin throat would belch forth." Onomatopoeia: "The notched edge of a small saw; it flashed and squealed: squee-squee-squee." "Trrr, his heels went, as they dragged across the rug; and the carpet was covered with little wrinkles."

POETIC IMAGERY

Imagery abounds throughout the novel. Often, I'm reminded of the *Gormenghast* trilogy (1946) by Mervyn Peake where characters and scenes are distorted, larger than themselves. Bely focuses strongly on mankind. First a simile: "Began to extract him like a sack stuffed full of goods." Then a gruesome metaphor: "Man, as is well known, is slush sewn up in skin." And man can look pitiful. "Likhutin was dressed in civilian clothes, and they sat on him like a saddle on a cow." Mirrors play a significant part in Bely's imagery. "The shattered spray of the mirrors, like a delicate spider's web." They become personified. "The mirrors were now merrily gleaming: and all the mirrors began to laugh." "The mirror cracked with loud laughter: across it like lightning a crooked needle flew with a gentle crunching sound; and froze there forever in a silvery zigzag."

Other objects grow a life of their own. "A statue by Itelli, which stretched its fingers into the closing day." "A court carriage carrying bright red lamps that looked like bloodshot eyes." It is almost as if the body parts were separate objects. "His fingers that raced over the keys, pouring out runs; the treble danced all over the place and the bass sluggishly ground into motion."

"The tooth of time should not gnaw them away with snow, rain and frost." "Noses flowed past in large numbers: aquiline, duck-like, cockerel-like, greenish, white: here also flowed the absence of any nose at all." "Like a bloody cloud, plumes lowered, Hussars swept past on their grey chargers." "A colour that was connected with insomnia and white spring nights and September somber ones." "The lights of the shore were scattered like luminous grain; the many-eyed seashore bristled with reeds."

And weather plays a role also. "The storm clouds cut into the moon; the strands of witches' tresses flew over the sky." "The sky has begun to fill with a flood of heavy tin: September is no more." "Brightly the moon's transverse rays stretch like white rafters: you walk through them." "The unmerciful sunset sent blow upon blow from the very horizon itself; higher rose the immensity of the rosy ripples."

PETERSBURG

St. Petersburg dominates this novel because it became the major city of Russia since Peter the Great founded it in 1703. It was controversial being built on swampland beside the Baltic Sea. However, government as well as the arts flourished there. We will see how Bely brings this great metropolis to life in all times of day and all seasons.

"Petersburg pursued and chased with its cerebral play and tearful spaciousness. "The wealthy houses: "The golden pier-glasses in the window-piers devoured the drawing-room from all sides with the green surfaces of mirrors." "A beautiful staircase! And it has steps—as soft as the convolutions of the brain." "Cold was the drawing-room's hospitality." "They thickened into a yellowish smoke, pressing themselves against the roofs like a threat."

"The pavements whispered and shuffled—beneath a throng of stone houses like giants." "The night was black, dark blue and lilac, shading into the reddish blotches of the street lamps as into the fiery blotches of a fiery rash." "Couple after couple flowed past: threesomes, foursomes flowed past; from each one to the sky rose a smoky pillar of conversation." "The melodic voice of the motor car roulade, the yellow-and-red tramcar and the man-in-the-street of every kind."

Petersburg sat on the turbulent Neva River. "A dark stripe of soot rose high from the funnels of steamboats; and fell like a tail into the Neva." "The Neva seethed, and cried desperately." "A row of riverside street lamps dropped fiery tears into the Neva." Across the Neva on islands lived the poor. "Massive buildings of the islands rose, casting into the mists their palely shining eyes—infinitely, soundlessly, tormentingly: and they seemed to be weeping."

We notice an underlying tension and sadness in many of these descriptions. "Meanwhile a cold, whistling pandemonium had broken out along the Nevsky, swooping, rattling and whispering with small, staccato, steady drops against the umbrellas, the sternly bent backs, drenching the hair, drenching the frozen, stringy hands of artisans, students, and workers." "Shreds of bluish mist, from which drops squelched, spinning metallic bubbles on the surfaces of the gurgling puddles."

"The red leaves, knocking against the panes as they floated down, exchanged whispered secrets." One inspiration is the cranes flying above the city. "Somewhere, on Nevsky Prospect, let us suppose, in the quiver of the flying carriages and the uproar of the newspaper-sellers, where above it all perhaps only the throat of the motor car rises—among those metal throats, at a pre-vesperal, vernal hour."

APOLLON

Apollon is the major character in this novel, born into the upper class. He was bright and very hardworking, rising to be a high government official. Bely created him to show the difficulties the ruling powers faced. He "transferred the centre of his consciousness by will power from the departmental staircase to the doors of his office." When he spoke to groups "it was as if a velvet bumble-bee of enormous dimensions had begun to drone." He decimated his rivals. "These speeches did not explode, but flashing without thunder spurted a kind of poison on the opposing party."

"His face, a pale one, recalled both a grey paperweight (in solemn moments) and a piece of papier mache (in hours of leisure)." "His bald pate; the surface of the enormous cranium, as bare as a knee." However, he reached a point where the estrangement of his wife and overwork took its toll." Little bags of skin hung down offendedly from the corners of his lips." "His unshaven chin . . . studded all over with a dense and prickly, completely white stubble, as though by a hoar frost that had fallen overnight."

He had his nervous tics, "born for solitary confinement." He "did not like his spacious flat; the furniture there shone so tiresomely, so eternally: and when the covers were put on, the furniture in its white covers stood before the gaze like snowy hills." "He feared spatial expanses. He feared them more than zigzags, than broken lines and sectors; country landscape simply scared him: beyond the wastes of snow and ice."

"He really did feel like a bare, picked skeleton from which Russia had fallen away." He "let his hand drop; two yellow bones drummed distinctly on the card table." He felt like "a black, mouse-like heap." He began to burn his official papers. "From behind the nota benes, the question marks, the section marks, the dashes, from behind the work that was now the last, a death's head rose towards the fire in the hearth; its lips muttered of themselves."

However, his wife had returned and they had reconciled. "The very sound-combination 'Anna Petrovna' broke against his eardrums, like a firecracker thrown at a teacher from under a school desk." He and his son had not gotten along since Nikolai had been a child. "When both came into psychic contact with each other, they resembled two dark air vents turned face-to-face into a complete abyss." Now Apollon felt rejuvenated. He would learn from how Anna showed love for her son. Anna's "two arms stretched out: the face had aged, and the arms trembled in the lace of the gold street lamps, which had just been lit."

NIKOLAI

Nikolai, Apollon's only son, was also bright and grew up with all the amenities. Yet he could never focus on goals like his father. "The nobility in his face was manifested in a notable manner by his forehead—chiseled, with small, swollen veins." Since he studied so much in his room, his "robe, so to speak, extended into all the appurtenances of the room."

Often his studies left him confused. "After he had been reading those treatises every object, even more than that—every name of an object seemed to him inconceivable, and vice versa: everything conceivable proved to be completely insubstantial, without object." "Completely irrelevant, idle thoughts that like flocks of frenzied crows, frightened by a shot, rise from a tree with many boughs and begin to circle."

He traveled. "Within him the bag of Aeolus had burst, and the sons of far-off gusts had drawn him with whistling whips through the air to some strange lands." He had passionate affairs. "Feverish poison penetrated his brain, pouring invisibly out of his eyes like a fiery cloud, entwining him in clinging, blood-red satin." But he felt exhausted. "The overcoat fell down somehow sleepily."

Like his father he too became depressed. "His 'I' turned out to be merely a black receptacle, if not a cramped storeroom, immersed in absolute darkness." He "'felt that his skin did not enwrap his body, but . . . a heap of cobblestones; instead of a brain he had a cobblestone; and there was a cobblestone in his stomach." "From the corner, bubbling, burst quiet wheezings and a throat seemed to gurgle: a unique, cockerel-like, inhuman whisper."

Having lost all direction, he made a disastrous mistake by accepting a bomb to blow up his father's government building. "I turned the key; even, yes: began to sob, I assume you, like a drunken body, half awake, when it's shaken out of slumber." "The little lump twisted and bowed with a cowardly, grinning mouth." "There was a roar: he understood everything." Fortunately, it went off in a room of Nikolai's house hurting no one. "The open door continued to yawn amidst the everyday, opening in the everyday its un-every-day depth: cosmic immensity." If philosophy could not console him, perhaps his parents' newly refurbished love could.

LIPPANCHENKO AND ALEKSANDR

From humble origins but with brains and drive, Lippanchenko became a revolutionary leader. "The fair-haired, rosy, twenty-five-year-old Paris student—the student Lipensky—swelling up like a delirious dream, turned stubbornly into a forty-five-year-old, indecent spider's belly." "Lippanchenko's lips recalled little pieces of sliced-up salmon—not yellow-red, but buttery and yellow."

"Now he sat on the bed, hairy and naked, with his legs apart; female-like rounded shapes were clearly marked on his shaggy chest." But he had gentle moments. "The bloodthirsty beast seems meek and domesticated, displaying the good nature of which it, too, is capable." He is even loved. "Her anxious eyes very nearly leapt out of their sockets; anxiously they ran over the tablecloth, clambered up on to the fat chest and forced their way into the little, blinking eyes."

A nobleman Aleksandr, wanting the best for Russia, was persuaded by the glib Lippanchenko to perform evil deeds in the name of the revolution. Aleksandr felt brilliant and all-powerful when drunk. "His experiences trailed after him like a flying, power-laden tail." "He had only to sober up a little for the salt of brilliance to vanish off somewhere."

This unbalanced young man began to hallucinate and see a strange person in his room. "He looked like a sheet of dark, black paper, motionlessly stuck in the window frame . . . had plainly become a layer of soot on the moonlit pane." He "dreamed that this perforated shoe was a living creature; a domestic creature, perhaps, like a dog or a cat; it shuffled around independently, creeping about the room and rustling in the corners; when Aleksandr Ivanovich was about to feed it a piece of white bread he had chewed in his mouth, the shuffling creature had bitten him on the finger with its perforated opening."

In this manic state he focused on Lippanchenko as the origin of all his problems. He stalked him and stabbed him to death, the only death in this novel, at least on stage. The book does not tell us how many died in the revolution of 1905, that these characters instigated.

UNREST

Revolutions had taken place before the momentous Communist revolution of 1917. Indirectly in this novel we can sense the growing discontent of the Russian people. "That band of giants would soon shamelessly and brazenly bury in their attics and basements the whole of the islands' poor." "The rural distances will be muttering, whispering there, in the expanse." "There in those days the usual swarms were growing exceedingly and fusing one with another into a many-headed, many-voiced, enormous blackness."

"A creeping, wailing myriapod was there; into a single damp space multivarious voices were poured—a multivariety of words; articulate phrases broke there one against the other." "Breaking loose from the wooden pole, tearing the air with their crests, where they fluttered and snatched, flew the gently whistling blades of a red calico banner." "There was panic; from afar—above the heads there, blood seemed to gush; seething red crests unwound from the black soot, like throbbing lights and like deer's antlers."

"Ordinary men in the street long ago christened these arrows with a name: soap bubbles." These 'bubbles' were the many edicts and rulings the government handed down. "What for the wearer of diamond insignia was only the middle of life's wanderings turned out for so many high officials to be the ending of life's way." Many officials had been assassinated. And yet the political machine carried on. "The helpless circle of the revolution of our wheel of state."

"Russia, you are like a steed! Into the darkness, into the emptiness your two front hooves have raced; and firmly in the granite soil have struck root—your two back ones." This statue of Peter the Great meant a lot to the Petersburg people. A legend persisted that if the statue came to life and raced away, tragedy would befall Russia.

"The Bronze Horseman flew on into the fog; in his eyes was a greenish depth; the muscles of his metal hands straightened, tautened; and the bronze sinciput darted; the horse's hooves fell on the cobblestones, on the swift and blinding arcs; the horse's mouth split apart in a deafening neighing, reminiscent of the whistlings of a locomotive; the thick steam from its nostrils splashed the street with luminous boiling water."

"The lusterless metal cloak hung down heavily—from shoulders that were shot with brilliance and from armour that was like fish-scales; cast-metal lip melted and trembled ambiguously."

"With his metal rear the emperor cast in bronze resonantly clanged against a chair; his green elbow fell with all the heaviness of bronze on the cheap little table from under the fold of his cloak, with bell-like, booming sounds; and with slow absent-mindedness the emperor removed his bronze laurels from his head; and the bronze laurel crown fell, with a crash, from his brow."

ADDENDUM

Great literary works like *Ulysses* and *In Search of Lost Time* could be written in relative freedom in the early twentieth century in Western Europe. However, in Russia, first the Czars, then afterwards the Communists, tried to shape individual expression. Andrei Bely suffered great hardship in his brief life (1880-1934). That was why his novel—such a poetic celebration of life—was prosecuted during his lifetime and took so long to reach the West in English translation.

As a conclusion, I would like to share some of Bely's philosophical insights that can be stunning:

"Wringing their cold fingers in an access of fruitless obsequiousness."

"Crossing infinity, without the slightest murmur—in the infinite stream of others like himself—among the flight, the hubbub, the trembling."

"Consciousness, detaching itself from the body, like the handle on the lever of a machine, starts to revolve around the whole organism, making everything incredibly clear."

"The vain hope that world is reality and that it is not a howling limitlessness."

"Like a wretched little vessel that is rigged with words and gestures that are completely expressible; but if the wretched little vessel happens to run aground on the underwater rock of life's incoherence, then the wretched little vessel, having run aground on the rock, falls to pieces."

"We often drink coffee with cream over the abyss."

Eric Greinke

SPEAKING FOR EVERYONE

"This is the beginning—from 'I' to 'we'."
—John Steinbeck

The majority of the poetry published today is on the Internet, available all over the world to anyone with computer access. Audiences are no longer restricted by limited geographical and national boundaries. Given the globalization of communication, the arts, like everything else from science to fashion, must adjust to the new reality of a much more widespread dissemination.

A kind of poetry that has thus far been uncommon but that is particularly well-suited to the new international literary scene is the personal-plural, hereafter called the "we" poem. This approach has an anthropocentric focus and a collective voice/persona. In this mode, a poet or poets speak for all of us as a species.

It's quite idealistic, I know, but the alternative seems to be fatalistic nihilism, so I, an old man, choose idealism. Nothing ventured, nothing gained.

Websters defines *egocentrism* as "viewing everything in relation to oneself, self-centered." *Ethnocentrism* is defined as "the belief that one's own ethnic group, nation or culture is superior." *Anthropocentrism* is defined as a belief "that considers human kind as the central focus, conceiving of everything in terms of human values."

Each of these centric belief systems has a correlate/analogue in poetry and the other arts. Critic Robert Peters, in his book *Hunting the Snark: A Compendium of New Poetic Terminology*, wrote "The ego poem, or the "I" poem, is the genre favored by most poets today, and especially by the younger products (Yes, poetry in this country is big business) of our ubiquitous writing programs." My old friend Donald Hall famously referred to them as "McPoems".

In terms of greater relatability and accessibility, ethnocentric poems are more universal than ego poems. Ethnocentrism is a step above and away from self-centered McPoems toward greater generalization. "Not just me, but others who are *like* me" is the idea. When considering the whole of humankind, however, ethnocentrism leads to polarization and, ultimately, conflict. Ethnocentrism is ultimately incompatible with a general humanism.

The Anthropoetic mode is not necessarily one that poets need to occupy full time. Anthropoetics is a movement of poems, not poetry. Maybe a single poet would "only" write one poem in her lifetime that spoke directly for the human species. That, combined with the unique Anthropoetic poems of others, would promote conceptual and emotional bonding between people around the world. This would be a better goal for poets to pursue than personal aggrandizement. I hope poets and other artists will be open to that part of themselves that connects us all, and to expressing it.

Greater universality may be achieved through a more depersonalized (thus more generalized) persona. The personal element, on a superficial level, tends to distract from the universal when it is too specific to the poet's particular experience and not fully connected to that deeper level that represents common experience. Historically, the Deep Imagists and the Surrealists were heading in this direction. Objectivism also demonstrated a more universal approach. In the nineteen-thirties, socialist American poet Walter Lowenfels proposed that poetry should be published anonymously. Lowenfels followed his own advice for a time, before dropping out of the literary scene completely for sixteen years to become a union organizer. Lowenfels, in addition to poetry, edited several international anthologies, including *Where Is Vietnam?—American Poets Respond* (Doubleday Anchor, New York, NY, 1967) and *For Neruda/For Chile* (Beacon Press, Boston, MA, 1975). I knew him during the last few years of his life. Our correspondence was largely focused on the social responsibility of the poet. Here's one of Lowenfels' poems that addresses the Big Picture.

I Belong

There are three billion billion billion constellations
    (the sky books says) but I am a patriot of the
    Milky Way. It gives me a thrill when I look
    out the telescope at *our* galaxy. I mean—I
    know where I belong—just like those two tit-
    mice feeding together outside my window, and
    right now flying off together—I, too, know
    I have a home, an identity established not
    only by national boundaries, common speech,

etc., not just by our own beautiful sun, and
its planets, moons, asteroids, but by our own
dear galaxy. O lover
in your pure feathery light, across thousands of billions
of spiral nebulas, you are the best of all
galaxies
and I know you love me too, for out of the vast riches
of your fiery interstellar sperm you have
given me inalienable rights to life, liberty
and the pursuit of happiness
and my own little life to cool.

"I Belong" is a confirmation and recognition of the energy that connects all life. It's a good example of how simple language and imagery can be used to impart a deeper meaning.

Incredibly, it seems that the idea of anonymity does not have a strong appeal to the majority of poets, the conveyers of the ego poems. Strange, but true! The idea of poetic anonymity is a radical step in the direction of a less personalized persona. Ironically, the early imagists thought that the image, by itself, could carry the meaning of the poem as well as lessen the selfish presence of the poet. They placed high value on specificity and description, which too often buried the metaphor and its meaning with the poem becoming cluttered with fussy detail that confounded or distracted the reader. Poets struggled to find "the right word" and that often seemed to become a priority in and of itself. In essence, their "rich" imagery too often camouflaged a lack of meaning.

I've been discussing the idea of collecting an anthology of "we" poems for the past couple years with several contemporaries, most notably Jim Cohn (Colorado Poet, disability advocate and curator of the Museum of Modern Poetics), Gary Metras (Poet Laureate of Easthampton, MA and publisher of Adasta Press), and Peter Krok (Philadelphia's red brick poet, Arts Archivist and Editor of *SVJ*). It was Peter who suggested that an essay or two might clarify the goals and parameters of our project. My first attempt was published as "Anthropoetics" in *SVJ* Vol. 52. In this one, I use examples from contemporary practice to further explicate the collective potential of the "we" poem to benefit mankind.

One of the best examples of a poem written as the result of a collective consciousness is "Echoes" by Peter Krok. As it's well known in Philadelphia, Peter

spends his days empowering other artists as the Director of the Manayunk
Roxborough Arts Center. A "we" poem is an expression of species consciousness, great empathy for others and unselfishness on the part of the poet.

Echoes

We take apart what took so long
to put together, like children
playing on carpets with tinker toys,
but we are not children. The years
now have their own stairway and
nooks of time we never left.
We have seen age wear away the face
that was our face and set before us
another outline in the looking glass.
The lines under the eyelids, you say,
were not expected, and I ask,
for there still are questions
what, after all, did we expect?

There are only the old addresses
and the echoes like the sound
still ringing in the seashell.
The past, like the tide, comes back.
Memory evokes the wanted image
which will not be left behind.
So was it under the August sun
when, like and Egyptian figurine,
with up-raised arms you held
the orange globe of dawn.
Your body in the Atlantic summer
all bronze and scented with the salt
of ocean spray returns continually.

Krok begins with a "we" that may be taken generally but progresses in the
last seven lines to a specific experience shared with one other person. By the
time the reader reaches "So was it under the August sun" the sense of general
inclusion is already established, so it lingers to the end and enhances reader
identification and thus the poems universality.

The following poem by Charles Fishman is a beautiful example of the use of primal language that translates easily and in which the imagery is universal. (Fishman has a wide international perspective, reflected in both his work as a poet and as an anthologist. He is poetry editor of *Prism: An Interdisciplinary Journal for Holocaust Educators* and, with Smita Sahay of Mumbai, India, is co-editing *Veils, Halos and Shackles: International Poetry on the Abuse and Oppression of Women.*)

Snow is the Poem Without Flags

for Orhan Pamuk

What is whiter than stars yet darker
than cloud-sifted moonlight, softer
than the breast that nurtures a child?

Only snow answers this call to mystery
and pleasure — the white snow of a winter's
morning   that dreams itself gone.

And what is its name, this creature
of cold light and desire, where is the center
of its knowledge and longing? Clearly, its address

is history and the heart its blue-white body,
but who can tame it and raise it up from silence?
who can instruct its paws to brush like lamplight

against her face? Only the white breath of the wind
— the wind that moans in Arabic and Turkish   in Hindi
and Hebrew   and English   in the cold mouth

that prays in a thousand tongues and knows
no mother or father   that cries like a child
who thirsts for the breast   only the wind

brushing the face of the snow that was born
anonymous   the wind in the snow's
white hair   And where can we find this snow,

immersed as we are in summer   in the heat
of war   with a hot sun blazing   and the whine
of rockets and bombs that fly like blown flakes

> of darkness   everything on fire with a great
> and unquenchable thirst? Only the wind can speak
> and name its country.

Fishman uses the common images of snow and wind to contrast with "the heat of war." The poem is easily translatable to other languages because it uses public symbols that are universally recognizable.

Poems have greater universal value when they are written in a collective voice. Lowenfels suggested that poets write anonymously, while others have suggested that we rise above the 1st person singular and avoid the use of "I." While the intention of such an approach is good, it isn't necessary to put such a radical restriction on poets, who should always be free to express themselves however they want. A better approach would be to mean "we" when writing "I." Poets should ask themselves to what degree their "I" is representative of the shared human condition. It's free to ask and good to know, because a poem's degree of universality is likely to be its greatest value. This poem by David Chorlton progresses from the "we" of a personal relationship to a wider, universal "we." (Chorlton comes to his world view through his life experiences. He was born in Austria and grew up in Manchester, England. He moved to Vienna in 1971. Seven years later, he married and moved to his wife's hometown of Phoenix, Arizona.)

Lost

> Once we had two silver teaspoons
> but they proved too small to control
> so now there's only one, while the set of forks
> that started as six became four
> and we're mystified as if
> two of them melted in dishwater. At the end
> of every wash a single blue sock
> lies crying out for its mate and now
> the tax forms have gone into hiding
> among papers we always meant to throw away
> but allowed to pile up on the desk,
>
> beside the stove, and on the table. We prefer
> not to think about the ring with a precious stone

that rolled through a crack in the floorboards
to a place we daren't go to look.
The catalogue of losses grows
as we blunder along, breaking this and mislaying
that. We lost the cozy lodge we used to stay at
when a sports bar took its place,
we lost the old houses on the corner of our street
to an office block, we lost
a mid-sized city to the huge one that replaced it.
We lost listening to the radio
for a friendly voice, we lost whole portions of the desert,
and we lost the gravel roads that led
to secret places when they were paved.
We lose some lions every year. We lose forests.
We lost the freedom to reclaim them. It's happening
all the time; a tree falls, a condor dies from eating
a poison carcass. We know where things belong;
the letters in a drawer, the cinnamon in a cupboard,
the pine trees on the mountain, but they're gone
like the glacier that shone for thousands of years, gone
like the shirt that opened out its sleeves
and flew miraculously away.

Chorlton skillfully transitions from personal losses to more general losses with the line "We lose some lives every year. We lose forests." His language is simple and direct, yet it invites the reader in through common experiences.

One may also begin with a highly generalized voice, as Alan Britt does in the next example. I met Alan in the early seventies when both of us first entered the literary scene in our early twenties. We shared an interest in the symbolist and surrealist artistic movements and Alan was especially passionate for South American surrealism. His mentor (Duane Locke) and mine (Robert Bly) advocated for the deep image approach, wherein poets try to dredge images up from their common human experience. Both of us incorporated the use of the "we" poem into our work early, despite the fact that hardly anyone wrote from a species-wide perspective. Throughout his poetry career, Alan has continued his interest in South and Central American poetry. Here is one of his poems that addresses the human connection:

We Are You

We rise on jaguar wings orbiting
a bronze waist before crossing
the torch of Liberty.

We sling ruthless reds, bruised
golds & tropical greens across
hurricanes chewing the Atlantic
coast off Cuba.

We surface the Amazon
with webbed toes.

Freedom's eyeglasses fogged we
enter each holy house as though
entering a proverbial hall of
mirrors,
aware the moon nursing Manhattan
skyscrapers also splinters the icy
peaks
of Peru, ignites Caymans in
Columbia,
the Quichua in Ecuador, yucca
lightning
in Mexico, plus Bolivar's bones in
Venezuela.

We chase amnesia thermals,
sometimes,
but mostly we prefer heirloom
tomatoes,
lean meats, exotic spices,
multigrain
& a dozen-year-old California
Syrah
after an exhausting day of painting
our
dreams across a canvas called
America.

Britt draws a common connection between the lives of both North and South Americans in a poetic call to international brotherhood in this poem.

Collaboration between two or more poets can also be an expressway into the "we" poem. I have collaborated extensively with poets old and young, male and female, and written about it in my book *The Third Voice: Notes on the Art of Poetic Collaboration*. Here are the first few sentences from that book: "When poets collaborate, the persona of their poems transmutates into a third voice, which is the combination of their individual voices. The poem they produce together is no longer a product of a single personality. It takes on a social aspect, even within the limitations of a duo."

Alison Stone and I wrote the following poem together. The title, "Emergency," is meant to have a double meaning. It asks if we can emerge from our state of limited empathy. The voice in the poem progresses from "I" to "we." Stone, a professional psychotherapist, is the author of several individual collections.

Emergency

A siren blares down the highway,
hysterically red as raw meat.
I imagine the worst disasters,
twisted bodies in crumpled cars,
stray bullets near a playground,
families trapped and screaming
or their houses on fire.
Next I think of real people,
then I hope it isn't them.

Sure, every victim is somebody's
something, but horror happening
to strangers is bearable, not
even as real as small annoyances
like running out of potato chips
during your annual Superbowl Party.
Maybe that's what it means to be
human, stuck in personal hungers,
ignoring or pretending to care

about everyone else,
one nation under fear
with justice for none.
Though we go through
the motions skillfully, and
even the siren's volume
is less than the scream of greed,
we wish for the silent strength
to somehow be more than our
natures, to match the siren's wail
with our authentic grief, to stand
alive and open in the red-tinged light.

I overheard a conversation at breakfast in a local café awhile back. They were discussing the pros and cons of vaccinations. Exasperated, the presumptive wife exclaimed, "I can't pretend to speak for everyone, but I think it's the apathy of guys like you that is killing a lot of people!" The man answered softly, but stubbornly "I don't care." It made me think of the old Pete Seeger song "Which Side Are You On?"

The post-modern literary taboo against the use of public symbols is a perverse denial of the natural function of literature as it is practiced and represented in world literature. As humans we share the symbolic archetypes that vary only slightly and superficially across all human culture. In terms of subjects for literature in general and poetry in particular, the "big subjects" of life, love, birth, death, courage, hope and faith are the human essence of poetry. A superficial value such as style pales by comparison to a poems essential content. Poets who want to achieve greater universality in their poems may want to utilize public symbols. Here's one of my poems that I hope expresses the human condition through use of common symbols:

Wings

The ocean cannot be contained,
but it can be heard inside a small shell.
Stars we named after ancient Gods
enter & depart in a dream.

They reverberate through
our collective neurons,
back beyond the big bang,
to an infinitesimal compact
of impacted selves,
their endings encoded in
expanding beams of energy.
We move toward the unknown,
blind in every dimension
but our poor human senses.
It's time to pack our weary trunks
for a much colder climate,
to share each other's warmth
like stranded survivors of an avalanche.
Molecules material but mortal,
beam to black space as errant waves,
each atom alone but connected,
quarking indeterminate but immanent.
Sweet orgasmic magic of our imaginations
plays on all the pages & stages of our days.
We take a break for the sake of sanity,
as they speak to us, through us & for us.
Then we cast them into the frozen fire,
transformed again into invisible wings.

The best poems speak to and for humanity. In the context of the widespread alienation, polarization and narcissism of the Age of Social Media, the realistic potential of an Anthropoetic movement may seem hopelessly idealistic. But, isn't it better to light one candle than to curse the darkness?

In whatever mode a poet chooses, including a first-person narrative, the potential for universality depends on the poet's ability to connect with the common human level of his consciousness. Poets should try to go as deeply into the universal subconscious as possible. The universal voice is a discovery, not an invention. Expanded ego-boundaries increase humanitarian awareness.

Reading "Wings" to audiences familiar with my work, someone usually comments that it "doesn't sound like" me. I'm happy to hear that, because I want it to sound like *us*.

Sources

The Grapes of Wrath, John Steinbeck, Viking Press, 1939

Hunting the Snark: A Compendium of New Poetic Terminology, Robert Peters, Paragon House, 1989

In The Path of Lightning, Charles Ades Fishman, Time Being Books, 2012

Invisible Wings, Eric Greinke, Presa Press. 2019

Looking for an Eye, Peter Krok, Foothills Publishing, 2008

Masterplan: Collaborative Poems, Eric Greinke and Alison Stone, Presa Press, 2018

Reading T.S. Eliot to a Bird, David Chorlton, Hoot n Waddle, 2018

Some Deaths: Selected Poems, 1925-1962, Walter Lowenfels, Nantahala Foundation, 1964

The Third Voice: Notes on the Art of Poetic Collaboration, Eric Greinke, Presa Press, 2017

Jeffrey Feingold

THE SUGAR THIEF

My Aunt Millie was a thief. She was large and loving, warm and wonderful. She was a little short, with a build like a potato. A potato with a large crop of curly orange hair on top. She loved conversations, hugs, and children. As a young boy, I loved when she wrapped me in her arms and gave me a big wet smooch on my cheek, leaving on my white-as-snow Eastern European face two perfect red lipstick imprints that Andy Warhol would have envied. Then she'd whisk me into her kitchen and insist on fattening up her skinny nephew with a homemade chopped liver and onion sandwich, glass of whole milk, and homemade macaroons to die for.

Aunt Millie and Uncle Joe lived in a beautiful white three-story house in an upscale Boston neighborhood. They drove an enormous white Cadillac with red leather seats, at a time when Americans drove either a Ford or a Chevy (my father was a confirmed Ford man), unless they were well off, in which case they drove a Cadillac. They summered in Boston and wintered at their home in Florida. Their origins were humble, but Uncle Joe had found success with his television shop. He sold TVs, at a time when one went to a TV shop in order to purchase a TV. There were no big box stores of any kind. If you wanted meat, you went to see the local butcher. If you wanted fruit and vegetables, you went to the local shop for those. And if you wanted one of those new-fangled boxes for family entertainment, you went to see Uncle Joe. The TVs back then had heavy lead glass in front of the tubes inside—the better to separate you from the radioactivity buzzing around the mysterious array of circuits and tubes and whatnot. My, how things have changed!

I admired Uncle Joe and adored Aunt Millie. But the darker truth is that she was often an embarrassment during my teenage years. She had lived through the Great Depression, and later, World War II, and the memory of those dark days was always with her. When we went out for lunch at the local diner, there were always sugar packets in a little ceramic holder on the table when we arrived. But they weren't there by the time we left. Sometimes I would return to our table after a bathroom visit, only to find the sugar had mysteriously disappeared from the table during my brief absence. Worse was when Aunt Millie would open her white leather pocketbook and start putting in the sugar packets, while I was still at the table eating. I would roll my eyes. What an embarrassment—my aunt stealing sugar from the diner! I could have died. In my youthful foolishness I imagined I was always being looked at—and judged—and that the world always cared about me and what I and my foolish old relative was doing. Had Aunt Millie also surreptitiously slipped some of the flatware into her cavernous pocketbook while I wasn't looking, I wondered? Wasn't there another teacup on the table when we'd arrived?

After years of her culinary crimes, I finally asked her why she took sugar packets with her. She explained how rationing had worked during the Depression and later during WWII. No one could buy sugar in unlimited quantities at the market. She would instead take her ration book to the market and exchange one of the stamps in the book for her half pound of sugar. Sugar was the start, but the rationing extended later to coffee, gasoline, butter, canned milk. Even jams, jellies and cooking oil became subject to rationing. Of course, a black market developed, and criminals got involved. I'd always known her sister's husband was a member of the Jewish mob, and as Aunt Millie explained about rationing, I imagined my maternal grandfather bartering in bootlegged butter before he was, later, rubbed out. But that's a story for a previous essay.

Now that I am in the September of my years, how I regret my youthful intolerance. How I wished I hadn't judged my beloved Aunt so harshly for her sweet thievery. But back then, I found all my familial elders embarrassing. They are mostly gone now, dead these many years. If only I could revive them. I pine for missed conversations. I want to greet all my many dead relatives, to welcome them into my house, to sit together with them at my kitchen table, have a cup of coffee, and listen to their stories. To see their eyes and smiles and to hear their sighs and laughter once more. I know they would then have to return to being shades, for life is not for the dead. Still, I want to sit at the kitchen table and listen to my Uncle Joe talk about the latest in black and white televisions, to hear my grandmother Frances' lilting laugh, and to see my Aunt Millie's broad smile and crop of curly orange hair,

and to feel only love and admiration when I return to my kitchen table to find all the sugar packets have mysteriously vanished into thin air. And she would be right to take them, for no matter what your success in life, the darkness is still there. I failed to grasp that as a youth. I wish I hadn't been embarrassed by her humanness. I wish I could shake that stupid young man I was by the shoulders and tell him so many things.

Nina Capille Oppenheim

EMILY, LOST IN THE WOODS

I felt myself moving toward a fairly predictable road in life: sleepless nights, the softest skin, dirty diapers, baby lotion. After nine months of carrying our baby, the road of parenthood was fully in view. We could see the path lined with our future—bassinet, stroller, two become three, how best to bring up baby. And then the road was gone. Just after forty weeks, the length of a full-term pregnancy, we lost her. And then we were floating, untethered, no road, no known path, lost in the woods.

In the early days our apartment was filled with flowers and sweet, sad messages from friends. They made a difference and they were kind and gentle and generous. All but one which read, "pick yourself up, dust yourself off and start all over again." Had the sender known that we had delivered a nine pound baby? Did they know about the 24 inch casket in the ground? We didn't know anyone who had lost a baby like this. There were no books. There was no guide. So how do you live? How do you find your way?

The shock of spring was bewildering. My inner life was so dark that I could not make sense of the beauty of the season. Pink blossoms on blooming cherry trees were a thing of unaccountable beauty. The surprise of life, of time marching on very slowly became less of an assault and more of a dull, longstanding ache. It was punctuated in that first year by the surprise of Mother's Day, a day which I'd only experienced as my mother's child; then my 38th birthday, then Christmas.

We found out that there could be laughter in sorrow. Was that even allowed? It appeared like a sprung jack-in-the-box and disappeared quickly, folded up in our rewritten narrative again. Like the time in the earliest days, when I was doing everything advisable to stop the flow of breast milk that had no outlet. My best friend brought ice packs—I was using them around the clock and milk still streamed down my body in the shower. She brought everything she could find in the drugstore. But she had the most hope for a knee pack, large and round and with a small hole cut out in the middle. She said that hole was the perfect place for my nipples so they wouldn't get freezer burn. We laughed in the way best friends do with a girls-only secret and the laughter kept coming up again and again.

Or like the day my husband and I visited the graves—when we buried our girl, we had bought our own plots, each of us flanking her on either side.

We had visited nearly every month that first year. One day we were surprised to see fresh, upturned earth and a new headstone immediately next to my future assigned spot. The shock of this—that someone had had the audacity to die and lay beside me and lay so closely—at first seemed inhumane. We looked closer at the neighbor's headstone. Apparently he had been a school bus driver. An etching of his portrait appeared on the stone so we could even see his face. The initial shock must have been about being confronted with our own mortality. The feeling passed quickly. I threw up my hands and said to my husband. "I hope he's a good bedfellow". We cried with laughter in the empty-life field.

There was something else more memorable than the tragic laughter though. The other stories, the other names. Our dear friends in Japan. A family friend in Ohio. A stranger from Spain. A previously anonymous colleague who had lost a boy named Michael. A childhood friend who lost her Logan at the end. A baby named Madeline. An unnamed would-have-been uncle. Nearly all of them stillborn. We were connected by loss to these people and to every generation in the history of woman and man.

Self-pity was always beckoning me to cry, to stay in bed, to give up. My husband's rallying instinct to "make meaning out of this" was the only thing that kept me from falling into the pit. We held on to each other and tried to figure it out. How do you love someone who isn't there? How do you go on when the path crumbles at your feet? How do you live?

Shaun Bailey is the author of *Mud Puddlers*, a 2018 finalist for The National Indie Excellence Book Awards. He was born and now works in Flint, Michigan, yet he spent much of his career working in the Delaware Bayshore region. As a result, his writing often juxtaposes boomtowns and the environment within the literary subgenre of rural noir.

Deborah Bayer is a retired Infectious Diseases physician. Her poems have appeared in *U.S. 1 Worksheets, Juked, Levee Magazine, The Stillwater Review, Cider Press Review,* and in the anthologies *Still You: Poems of Illness and Healing* (Wolf Ridge Press) and *More Challenges for the Delusional* (Diode Editions). Her chapbook *Rope Made of Bandages* is forthcoming from Finishing Line Press. She is pursuing a Certificate of Professional Achievement in Narrative Medicine from Columbia University.

Joe Benevento is the author of fourteen books of poetry and fiction, including: *Expecting Songbirds: Selected Poems, 1983-2015,* with the Purple Flag imprint of the Visual Artists Collective. His work has appeared in close to 300 publications, including *Prairie Schooner, Poets & Writers, Cold Mountain Review, I 70 Review and Bilingual Review.* He teaches creative writing and American literature at Truman State and is poetry editor for the *Green Hills Literary Lantern.*

A recent graduate of Rutgers-Newark's MFA program, **John Blahnik** teaches writing at Montclair State University and lives in Manhattan with his wife and newborn son.

Nina Capille-Oppenheim grew up on the farms and beaches of Atlantic County, NJ, rowed the Stotesbury Regatta on the Schuylkill River with Atlantic City High School's Lightweight 8 and is currently a MFA candidate at CUNY's City College (Creative Writing/Fiction). She lives in New York City with her family.

Michael J. Carter is a poet and psychotherapist living in Vermont. He holds an MFA from Vermont College and an MSW from Smith. His poems have appeared in journals such at *Western Humanities Review, MomEgg, Ploughshares,* and *Sixth Finch,* among many others.

Joseph Chelius has contributed poems to such journals as *Commonweal, Poet Lore, Poetry East, Rattle,* and *THINK.* He has published two full-length collections of poetry with WordTech editions: *The Art of Acquiescence* (2014) and *Crossing State Lines* (2020).

Marisa P. Clark is a queer writer whose prose and poetry appear in *Shenandoah, Cream City Review, Nimrod, Epiphany, Foglifter, Free State Review, Rust + Moth, Texas Review, Sundog Lit,* and elsewhere. Best American Essays 2011 recognized her creative nonfiction among its Notable Essays. She also reads fiction for *New England Review.*

Mike Cohen hosts Poetry Aloud and Alive at Philadelphia's Big Blue Marble Book Store. His articles on sculpture appear in *Schuylkill Valley Journal* to which he is a contributing editor. Mike has memorized a good deal of his poetry, having found that while some poems should be seen and not heard, others should be heard and not seen. It is a constant struggle to keep them sorted properly and to keep poems that should be neither seen nor heard out of the mix. Constant companion, cohabitant, cohort, and confidante, Connie, keeps Mike and his poems from getting off-kilter. Mike's wry writing has appeared in the *Mad Poets Review, Fox Chase Review,* and other journals. His poetic presentations feature humor and drama against a philosophical backdrop. Look for him at http://mikecohensays.com, on YouTube, and in his book, *Between the I's* as well as the forthcoming collection of poems and short tales, *Between the Shadow and the Wall.*

Jessica de Koninck is the author of one full length collection, *Cutting Room* (Terrapin Books) and one chapbook, *Repairs* (Finishing Line Press). Her poems appear in numerous journals and anthologies. A four-time Pushcart Prize nominee, she was a winner of the *Writer's Almanac Pandemic Poetry Contest.* Her work has been featured on *Verse Daily,* and her poems and manuscripts were finalists in the Raynes, Dobler, Juniper Press and Black Lawrence competitions. www.jessicadekoninck.com

Jo Angela Edwins has published poems in various venues, including recently in *Breakwater Review, Twelve Mile Review,* and *Halfway Down the Stairs.* Her chapbook *Play* was published in 2016. She has received awards from Winning Writers, Poetry Super Highway, and the SC Academy of Authors and is a Pushcart Prize, Forward Prize, and Bettering American Poetry nominee. A resident of Florence, SC, she is the poet laureate of the Pee Dee region of the state.

L.S. Engler writes from outside of Chicago, though she grew up chasing dragons in the woods of Michigan. Her work has appeared in many anthologies and journals, including *Pulp Modern, Phantaxis, Bards and Sages Quarterly,* and *The Saturday Evening Post.*

Dan Farkas is an itinerant New Yorker currently exiled in Cleveland. His joys in life come from creative writing, photography, Elton John, Steely Dan, his wife and kids, and sometimes the NY Rangers. His latest published pieces are "Summer's End on Erie" in *The Birdseed Magazine* and "Ascension Song" and "The Wedding Toast" in *The Prompt Magazine.*

Jeffrey Feingold is a writer in Boston, MA. He has workshopped essays with GrubStreet. His essays "The World of Tomorrow" and "The Wrong Napkin" were accepted for publication in April, 2022 in *Wilderness House Literary Review.* His essay "Avalanche" was published by *Impspired* magazine (online in Feb., 2022 and in print editions in May, 2022), and will also be published online by The Bark. "The Buzz Bomb" was first published by *Atticus Review,* and by *The Raven's Perch* in 2022. He is currently working on a book of essays, *Coffee With Ghosts.*

Ray Greenblatt published two books of poetry in 2020: *Until the First Light* (Parnilis Media) and *Man in a Crow Suit* (BookArts Press). He has also published flash fiction and book reviews. The Dylan Thomas Society, the John Updike Society, and the Graham Greene Society are the most recent publishers of his reviews. His work has been translated into Japanese, Polish, and Greek.

Eric Greinke has been active on the international literary scene since the early seventies. His poems and essays have been published in hundreds of magazines, most recently in *The American Journal of Poetry, Rosebud, North Dakota Quarterly, Trajectory* and the *Bryant Literary Review.* His book *For The Living Dead – Selected Poems* (Presa Press & Simon Pulse, 2014) has been downloaded over three million times and was nominated for a Pulitzer Prize and a National Book Award. His new collection of poetry is *Break Out* (Presa Press, 2020). He has worked in the Michigan Artists In The Schools Program and as a creative writing teacher at Grand Rapids City School, an experimental public school. He has also been an active reviewer of over one hundred poetry books over the past fifty years. www.ericgreinke.com

Grey's work appears in *Thrillist, Red Fez Publications,* and *Sledgehammer Lit.* She's taught English at the university and high school levels, but she currently makes a living as digital content creator for a traffic safety company. Her partner Katie and their dogs Juniper and Cashew frequent adventures in this unstable world.

Ann Howells edited *Illya's Honey* for eighteen years. Her recent books are: *So Long As We Speak Their Names* (Kelsay Books, 2019) and *Painting the Pinwheel Sky* (Assure Press, 2020). Chapbooks include: *Black Crow in Flight*, Editor's Choice in Main Street Rag's 2007 competition and *Softly Beating Wings*, William D. Barney Chapbook Competition winner (Blackbead Books, 2017). Ann's work appears in small press and university publications including *Plainsongs, I-70 Review*, and S*an Pedro River Review*.

Poet and songwriter **Paul Ilechko** is the author of several chapbooks, including *Pain Sections* (Alien Buddha Press). His work has appeared in a variety of journals, including *The Night Heron Barks, Feral Journal, K'in, Gargoyle Magazine*, and *Book of Matches*. His first album, *Meeting Points*, was released in 2021.

Keith Kopka is the recipient of the 2019 Tampa Review Prize for his collection of poems, *Count Four* (University of Tampa Press, 2020). His poetry and criticism has recently appeared in journals such as *Best New Poets, Mid-American Review, New Ohio Review*, and many others. Kopka is also the Director of Operations for *Writers Resist*, a Senior Editor at *Narrative Magazine*, and an Assistant Professor at Holy Family University in Philadelphia.

Koss has been published in many journals including *Bending Genres, Cincinnati Review, Chiron*, and others. They recently won the 2021 Wergle Flomp Humor Poetry Award with "My Therapist Sez." They received BOTN nominations in 2021 for fiction ("Bending Genres") and poetry ("Kissing Dynamite"). Keep up with Koss on Twitter @Koss51209969 and Instagram @koss_singular. Their website is http://koss-works.com.

Lavinia Kumar has published three books (most recently, *Hear Ye, Hear Ye: Women, Women: Soldiers, Spies of Revolutionary and Civil Wars*, and *No Longer Silent: the Silk and Iron of Women Scientists)* and four chapbooks (most recently, *Beauty. Salon. Art.*, Desert Willow Press, 2019). Her work is upcoming or recently published in *Decolonial Passage, Hole in the Head Review, Minerva Rising, Paterson Literary Review, River Heron Review, Superpresent*, & *SurVision*. Her website is laviniakumar.org.

Jane Rosenberg LaForge is the author of three full-length collections of poetry, four chapbooks, a memoir, and two novels. Her newest poetry collection is *Medusa's Daughter* (Animal Heart Press 2021). Her 2018 novel, *The Hawkman: A Fairy Tale of the Great War* (Amberjack Publishing), was a finalist in two categories in the Eric Hoffer awards. She reviews books for *American Book Review* and reads poetry for *Counterclock* literary magazine.

Christopher Locke's flash has appeared in such magazines as *SmokeLong Quarterly, Jellyfish Review, Barrelhouse, Flash Fiction Magazine, New Flash Fiction Review, Maudlin House, Noir Nation,* and elsewhere. He won the Black River Chapbook Award (Black Lawrence Press—2020) for his collection of short stories *25 Trumbulls Road.* He has been nominated for Best of the Net and The Pushcart Prize many times. Chris lives in the Adirondacks where he teaches English at North Country Community College.

Katharyn Howd Machan's most recent publications are *A Slow Bottle of Wine* (The Comstock Writers, Inc., 2020) and *What the Piper Promised* (Alexandria Quarterly Press, 2018), both winners in national chapbook competitions. Her poems have appeared in numerous magazines, anthologies, and textbooks, including *The Bedford Introduction to Literature* and *Sound and Sense.* A professor in the Writing Department at Ithaca College in central New York State, she served as Tompkins County's first poet laureate.

Adam Matson is the author of two collections of short fiction, *Sometimes Things Go Horribly Wrong* and *Watch City.* His fiction has appeared internationally in over thirty publications.

Bruce McRae, a Canadian musician, is a multiple Pushcart nominee with poems published in hundreds of magazines such as *Poetry, Rattle* and the *North American Review.* His books are *The So-Called Sonnets* (Silenced Press); *An Unbecoming Fit Of Frenzy;* (Cawing Crow Press) *and Like As If* (Pski's Porch), *Hearsay* (The Poet's Haven).

Devon Miller-Duggan has published poems in *Margie, The Antioch Review, Massachusetts Review,* and *Spillway.* She teaches at the University of Delaware. Her books include *Pinning the Bird to the Wall* (Tres Chicas Books, 2008), *Alphabet Year* (Wipf & Stock, 2017), *The Slow Salute* (Lithic Press Chapbook Competition Winner, 2018).

Kurt Olsson's work has appeared in a wide variety of publications, including *Poetry, The Threepenny Review, The New Republic,* and *Southern Review.* He has published two collections of poetry, *Burning Down Disneyland* (Gunpowder Press) and *What Kills What Kills Us* (Silverfish Review Press).

Alan Perry's debut chapbook, *Clerk of the Dead*, was released by Main Street Rag Publishing in 2020. His poems have appeared in *Tahoma Literary Review, Open: Journal of Arts & Letters, Ocotillo Review, Heron Tree, Remington Review*, among others, and in several anthologies. He is a founder and Co-Managing Editor of *RockPaperPoem*, a Senior Poetry Editor for *Typehouse Literary Magazine*, and a Best of the Net nominee.

John Reed is the author of three novels, one book of poetry, two non-fiction illustrated projects, one project of poetry/theater, and one book of history/narrative non-fiction; published in *Artforum, Art in America, the Believer, the PEN Poetry Series, Gawker, Slate, the Paris Review, the Times Literary Supplement, Vice, The New York Times, Rolling Stone, Harpers*; anthologized in *Best American Essays*; current faculty at The New School University MFA in Creative Writing.

Lynda Gene Rymond is the author of *The Village of Basketeers* and *Oscar and the Mooncats* (Houghton Mifflin.) She attended Bucks County Community College and received a BFA from the California College of Arts and Crafts. A runner-up or finalist for Bucks County Poet Laureate in 2019, 2020, and 2021, her poems have been published in multiple journals and the anthology, *Carry Us to the Next Well* (Kelsay Press.) She lives in Applebachsville, Pa.

Kelly R. Samuels is the author of the full-length collection *All the Time in the World* (Kelsay Books) and two chapbooks: *Words Some of Us Rarely Use* and *Zeena/Zenobia Speaks*. She is a Pushcart Prize and Best of the Net nominee with work appearing in *The Massachusetts Review, RHINO, The Carolina Quarterly, The Pinch*, and *Salt Hill*. She lives in the Upper Midwest.

Wendy Fulton Steginsky has authored three poetry books. In 2018 *Let This be Enough* (Kelsay Books, 2016) was awarded Honorable Mention in Bermuda's Literary Awards. She has co-edited two anthologies of poetry, *Carry Us to the Next Well* (2021) and *A Certain Kind of Swagger* (2022). In 2017 she was selected runner-up in the Bucks County, Pennsylvania Poet Laureate contest. She has been widely published in the Caribbean and the U.S.

Connie Swartzman held little regard for poetry for most of her life. She attributes this to less-than-talented English teachers who would lead the class on a dogged trudge, word by word, line by line, stanza by stanza, that ruined any natural appreciation the students may have possessed. This changed when she met her husband, poet and writer Mike Cohen, who inspired her toward a deep appreciation for poetry and to begin writing herself. In 2019, to her astonishment, she won first prize for poetry at the Philadelphia Writers Conference.

Joseph Howard Tyson graduated from LaSalle University with a B.A. in Philosophy, took graduate courses in English at Pennsylvania State University, then served in the U. S. Marine Corps. He lives in a Philadelphia suburb, and works in the insurance industry. In addition to non-fiction articles published in *Schuylkill Valley Journal, Southern Cross Review*, and other publications, he has written six books: *Penn's Luminous City* (2005), *Madame Blavatsky Revisited* (2006), *Hitler's Mentor: Dietrich Eckart* (2008), *The Surreal Reich* (2010), *World War II Leaders* (2011), and *Fifty-Seven Years of Russian Madness* (2015). Tyson is currently working on a satiric dictionary.

Lynne Viti is the author of *Dancing at Lake Montebello* (2020), *Baltimore Girls* (2017) and *The Glamorganshire Bible* (2018). Her fourth poetry collection, *The Walk to Cefalù,* is forthcoming from Cornerstone Press. She won honorable mentions in the Paterson Poetry Prize Contest, the WOMR-FM/Joe Gouveia Poetry Contest and the Fish Publishing Poetry Contest. A lecturer emerita at Wellesley College, she currently teaches in community programs and leads poetry workshops around Boston.

Andrew Vogel listens, walks the hills, and teaches in rural eastern Pennsylvania, the homelands of the displaced Lenape peoples. His poems have appeared *The Blue Collar Review, Poetry East, Off the Coast, Slant, The Evergreen Review, Parhelion, Hunger Mountain, Crab Creek Review, The Briar Cliff Review* and elsewhere.

John Wojtowicz's debut coffee-table-style chapbook *Roadside Attractions: A Poetic Guide to American Oddities* was published in 2022 by Parnilis Media. He serves as the Local Lyrics contributor for The Mad Poets Society Blog. John has been featured on Rowan University's Writer's Roundtable on WGLS-FM and several of his poems were chosen to be exhibited in Princeton University's 2021 "Unique Minds: Creative Voices" art show at the Lewis Center. www.johnwojtowicz.com

Robert Zaller is a poet, critic, and historian. His awards include a Guggenheim fellowship, and he is an elected member of the Royal Historical Society. His most recent verse collection is *Speaking to Power* (Moonstone Press). He is Drexel Distinguished University Professor of History Emeritus.

Schuylkill Valley Journal

—Submission Guidelines—

Schuylkill Valley Journal is published as both a print and online journal. *SVJ* print is released twice a year, in spring and fall. *SVJ* online (svjlit.com) is published on a more frequent basis. *SVJ* publishes short stories, flash fiction, interviews, photography, cityscapes, critical essays and features on art and sculpture (especially Philadelphia sculpture). *SVJ* also publishes poetry; however, all poetry will first appear in *SVJ* print.

All submissions (except poetry) should be sent through the website to svj.query@gmail.com. Please see separate information for poetry below. We prefer previously unpublished work though published work is acceptable (indicate where previously published). Simultaneous submissions are OK (please notify us if your work is published elsewhere). All submissions will be considered for both our print and online journals. Our aim in reviewing material that is first considered for *SVJ* online (material other than poetry and longer short stories) is to inform writers of the status of their inquiry within two weeks.

Submissions should be sent in .doc or .rtf file format only in Times New Roman, 12-point font, and single-spaced and should include title, author name, bio and complete text, including any notes regarding previous publication. In the subject line all submissions should state the submission type (e.g., short story, flash fiction, essay) and include the writer's full name, and contact information. Any file not meeting these specifications may not be read. Manuscripts will not be returned. All submissions except poetry should include a word count.

Poetry: Because of the volume of poetry we receive, our guidelines are more specific than other genres. Please read and follow carefully:

- We accept well-crafted/well-edited, accessible poetry, both free and formal verse in a variety of subjects and styles. We encourage you to read our journal and acquaint yourself with our general aesthetic before submitting.
- Send 3-5 poems in one document (.doc file format only—no zip files.)
- We prefer one poem per page (well-crafted longer poems accepted that will fit on no more than two pages of the print journal).
- No previously published poems. Unpublished work means work that has not appeared in any form of print or digital media, including books (self-published or traditional), journals, blogs, newspapers, personal webpages, or social media posts on your page or another.

- One submission per reading period. If we publish your poem(s) in our current issue, please wait a year (one submission period) before submitting again.
- Simultaneous submissions are fine providing that you let us know right away if your work is accepted elsewhere. Our goal is to respond within three to four months.
- Please include your last name and the words "Poetry Submission" in the subject line of your email.Send email to **2poetrysvj@gmail.com.**

Please Note: files should meet these guidelines and submission must be made during our open reading periods, or they will go unread.

Short Stories and Flash Fiction: 1-2 stories (if more than 3,000 words please only submit one). Flash fiction (preferably 500-1,000 words); short stories no more than 6,000 words. Submissions will be considered for both the online and print journal, with the exception of short stories greater than 2,000 words (*SVJ* print only). We like fiction that explores a situation or illuminates a character. We look for original use of language, fresh voices, and diversity. We also seek writers who have insights into the mysteries of everyday life, relationships and the world around us. Stories can pose questions and answer them or not; however, they must be well-crafted. Stories can be sent to **query.svj@gmail.com** or can be sent via snail mail. The preferred method is via snail mail. Stories sent by snail mail should be typed, double-spaced, one side only with name, address, word count and bio on first page. Send to:

Fran Metzman
Fiction Editor, *Schuylkill Valley Journal*
1900 JFK Blvd, /2012
Philadelphia, PA 19103

Essays and Interviews: 5,000 words max. (preferably under 2,000 words for *SVJ* on-line) on topics of literary or artistic interest, personal reflections, interviews, etc.). Submissions should incude the word count and bio on first page. Inquiry to email address (macpoet1@aol.com) is always advisable. Queries should include a concept/abstract of the proposed article, approximately a paragraph. All submissions will be sent through **query.svj@gmail.com.** All articles and non-fiction pieces will be assigned by editor.

Dispatches: Send 250-700 words + 50 word bio to **dispatchsvj@gmail.com** & feel free to add one link to your work / website that we will include with your bio. Dispatches is genre free. Whether it's beautiful or it's weird, we don't care as long as you keep it loose.

—Subscription Form—
Schuylkill Valley Journal

Name: _____

Street Address:_____

City, State, Zip Code:_____

Phone: _____

Subscriptions: ( ) One Year $33*   ( ) Two Years $58*
                    (includes postage)   (includes postage)

For an issue that contains my work:

( )   Send my payment copies with my subscription copy.

( )   Send my payment copies and transfer my subscription
      to the next issue.

Contributions

    ( ) $10   ( ) $25   ( ) $50   ( ) $100   ( ) Other

Please make checks payable to

    Peter Krok – *Schuylkill Valley Journal*

and mail to:

    Peter Krok, 240 Golf Hills Road, Havertown, PA 19083

*For subscriptions that do not require postage, a one year subscription is $30 and a two year subscription is $55.

Made in the USA
Columbia, SC
12 October 2022

68985280R00104